Sébastien Ronteau, Laurent Muzellec, Deepak Saxena, Daniel Trabucchi
Digital Business Models

Sébastien Ronteau, Laurent Muzellec,
Deepak Saxena, Daniel Trabucchi

Digital Business Models

The New Value Creation and Capture Mechanisms
of the 21st Century

DE GRUYTER

ISBN 978-3-11-076241-9
e-ISBN (PDF) 978-3-11-076255-6
e-ISBN (EPUB) 978-3-11-076259-4
DOI https://doi.org/10.1515/9783110762556

Library of Congress Control Number: 2022940112

Bibliographic information published by the Deutsche Nationalbibliothek
The Deutsche Nationalbibliothek lists this publication in the Deutsche Nationalbibliografie;
detailed bibliographic data are available on the internet at http://dnb.dnb.de.

© 2023 the author(s), published by Walter de Gruyter GmbH, Berlin/Boston
This book is published open access at www.degruyter.com.

Cover image: antoniokhr/iStock/Getty Images Plus
Typesetting: Integra Software Services Pvt. Ltd.
Printing and binding: CPI books GmbH, Leck

www.degruyter.com

This book is dedicated to my colleagues, friends, students and alumni at Audencia and Trinity Business School, who have sometimes been "guinea pigs" and often partners in passionate discussions regarding digital business models and digital entrepreneurs, and the way they are bringing a change to our world as well as the manner in which we interact.

I extend a tender and grateful thought to my companion and soul mate, Yasmine, and my amazing children, Antton and Lilas, for their patience and unfailing support when I locked myself in the attic to write these lines and many others. I love you.

– Sébastien Ronteau

This book is dedicated to my beloved wife Lisa, my beautiful children Lena, Barra and Killian and my dear sister, Anne-Francoise.　　　　　　　　– Laurent Muzellec

Dedicated to my dear parents, G.P. Saxena and Madhu Saxena, and my wife, Nisha.

– Deepak Saxena

This book is dedicated to the Irish adventure. Joining Trinity College in 2017 was a needed step in my PhD path, which turned out to be the beginning of a great friendship with Laurent and Seb. Meeting them through the rainy days that were spent writing various articles was an unexpected surprise that represents several different things today: our conference, our projects and this book, along with the many great moments spent together, and the memories we will continue to make. So, thank you, "Irish" friends – this book is dedicated to our great adventure together. . .and all the projects to come!　　　　　　　– Daniel Trabucchi

Preface

Every story has a context, a plot, and an ending. Behind the development of this book, there is a long story with several twists and turns, encounters, dead ends, joys and achievements.

I perfectly remember how it all began. At the time, I was not aware in the slightest that it would take up so much of my time and passion for years to come.

Laurent and I were enjoying coffee. He had just moved back to Ireland to develop a new master's in digital marketing. We had been already working together on one of our first articles on two-sided Internet platforms. In 2012, business models and the way the new companies were making money influenced our conversations and academic debates. Laurent is a professor in Marketing with a background in Political Science, whereas I am a professor in Entrepreneurship with a background in Economics, Strategy, and Innovation. Rather than sundering us, our discussions revealed the benefit of observing digital enterprises from different lenses: marketing, strategy, and entrepreneurship.

Laurent invited me to conduct a course on Digital Business Models in the newly launched MSc. No one seemed to have taught a module such as this one before. I was enthusiastic and started digging frantically for information in books, blogs, and academic articles. I found that knowledge in this area was scarce and disseminated over grey literature. Practitioners mainly focussed on business modelling while researchers seemed to be stuck on the traditional economic considerations.

The course was a success and has now been duplicated in Ireland and France. Needless to say, the Internet context changed; however, it is always challenging to train students and help them see beyond the consumer perspective to assess the strategic risks behind those well-known digital businesses that we admire for their success and the services they provide.

Along the way, we found companions and friends. Deepak, with his vast knowledge in Information Technologies, worked for Trinity Centre for Digital Business and Analytics. The centre, which was launched by Laurent, mirrors our desire for multidisciplinary research. Its goal is to foster multidisciplinary research to create and disseminate knowledge regarding digital business. Further interactions with CEOs and digital leaders fuelled our thoughts and ideas.

Daniel brought his background in Innovation Management as well as his intellectual enthusiasm for digital platform dynamics. He joined Trinity as a visiting PhD scholar from Politecnico di Milano. In the beginning, we were flattered as Daniel approached us regarding our joint paper, which had inspired him. We were then quickly impressed by his dynamism and prolific production on digital platforms. Daniel began several projects and invited us to contribute to some of the papers on the sharing economy, the value drivers behind digital businesses and the future of multi-sided platforms. We nurtured our passions on digital platforms through the *Symplatform*, an industry-academic symposium, which was initiated by Daniel:

Symplatform is the place where academic knowledge meets the practice world to foster a critical discussion on what platforms are, how they work and what they can become for people, organizations and our society.

Symplatform continues to influence a growing community around a yearly event and is now serving as a platform for its participants with different outlets, such as podcasts, books, MOOCs, and other initiatives.

Did I lose you? Why and how did we end up writing this book?

This book is a natural outcome of all the above. The pandemic was the opportunity to recall and realise this. Ultimately, it acted as an accelerator. We realised that we had the content from courses, case studies, conversations with digital leaders, a body of academic papers, and a team of individuals from different backgrounds who worked well together. Finally, we had found the energy and the time to settle our findings and views on Digital Business Models.

This book addresses how ventures design digital services to generate value. We adopt a strategic perspective to surpass the consumer perspective and analyse the business models at work in the digital arena.

The ambition is to give the readers a starting point – and hopefully much more – to address the complexity and a systemic perspective on the characteristics and implications of running a digital business. In addition, a business model as a concept is the perfect layer to recombine the rationales and logic of business actions underpinning a vision and a mission. It is not a listing of digital business models in a normative call. Rather, it is an open-ended perspective and personal thought on how we make sense of specificities and challenges of the best in class. For each chapter, we draw some "key takeaways and further considerations" for entrepreneurs, managers, and future digital leaders.

We hope that the same spark that drives us will touch you through your journey. **Enjoy your trip to Digital Business Models: New Value Creation and Capture Mechanisms of the 21st Century.**

S. Ronteau

About the Authors

Sébastien Ronteau is a professor of Entrepreneurship and co-head of the Hub for Exploration and Entrepreneurship at Audencia Business School. His research interests focus on Strategy, Entrepreneurship, and Digital Startups with a close look at Business models and ecosystems dynamics, as well as on entrepreneurial practices. His academic work has appeared in top-tier academic journals, such as *Entrepreneurship & Regional Development*, *Industrial Marketing Management*, *Internet Research*, and *Creativity and Innovation Management*. He is also an Adjunct Faculty at Trinity Business School, Trinity College Dublin, since 2017. He co-founded Symplatform in 2020. He advises start-ups and teaches digital business models and entrepreneurial business planning at executive levels.

Laurent Muzellec is a professor in Marketing and the founder and director of Trinity Centre for Digital Business and Analytics as well as the MSc in Digital Marketing Strategy at Trinity Business School, Trinity College Dublin. His research interests pertain to the field of digital business models, electronic Word of Mouth, and brand management. His articles have appeared in several international publications, including *Industrial Marketing Management*, *Marketing Theory*, *Journal of Advertising Research*, and *European Journal of Marketing*. Laurent teaches marketing strategy and digital marketing at the executive level, such as Executive MBA. He co-founded Symplatform in 2020.

Deepak Saxena is an Assistant Professor at the School of Management and Entrepreneurship, Indian Institute of Technology Jodhpur. He holds a PhD in Management Information Systems from Trinity College Dublin, Ireland. After obtaining his PhD, he worked with Trinity College Dublin as a research fellow in Digital Business, Dublin Institute of Technology as an assistant lecturer and Birla Institute of Technology and Science Pilani as an assistant professor. He has published his works in journals such as *Australasian Journal of Information Systems*, *Electronic Journal of Information Systems in Developing Countries*, *International Journal of Project Management*, *Irish Journal of Management*, *Journal of Information Science*, and *Journal of Information Technology Teaching Cases*, among others. He is currently serving as an associate editor for the *Electronic Journal of Business Research Methods* (Scopus-indexed) and serving on the review panel of more than ten internationally reputed Information Systems journals.

Daniel Trabucchi is an assistant professor in Innovation Management at the School of Management, Politecnico di Milano, where he also serves as a senior researcher in the LEADIN'Lab, Laboratory for LEAdership, Design and INnovation. He co-founded Symplatform, the symposium on digital platforms, which fosters discussions among scholars and practitioners. He is a scientific director at IDeaLs, a global research platform focusing on digital transformation processes. His research has been published in *Journal of Product Innovation Management*, *Technological Forecasting and Social Change*, *R&D Management*, *International Journal of Entrepreneurial Behavior and Research*, *Internet Research*, *Research-Technology Management*, and *Creativity and Innovation Management*.

Contents

Appendices: **Illustrative Case Studies**

1 Beyond Digital Ubiquity: The Digital Business Model Iron Triangle

We live in a digital world: digital services surround us in every moment of our daily lives. These devices, such as smartphones, have revolutionised the way we communicate, entertain ourselves, connect and form political opinions, as well as the way we look for information regarding products and services and how we buy and access them. Mobile phones have become more than another digital device since they are now used as an extension of ourselves. Not surprisingly, some of the most successful companies of our times, including Facebook, Google, and Apple, have managed to capitalise on their intimate access to and knowledge of the hyper-connected consumer. They have positioned themselves at the heart of the digital ecosystem, which provides them with unlimited reach to all of us, along with an ability to collect and harvest behavioural data about any end-user. These companies are trading on ubiquity, an omnipresent awareness of the customer and their journey. In this book, we surpass digital ubiquity to analyse how internet companies foster a digital business ecosystem and establish a sustainable competitive advantage by developing new revenue and business models. In this chapter, we contextualise this new digital environment, followed by contrasting the dynamics behind the success of the two transformative digital players – Netflix and Spotify – to illustrate how digital businesses can create, propose, deliver, and capture value. This leads us to propose an Iron triangle of a business model that echoes three key questions: Who is creating value? Which configuration (shape) does this value take? And finally, how sustainable is the competitive advantage?

1.1 Be Kind, Rewind

Let's stop the time, and rewind. Fifteen years ago, almost none of us had a smartphone – the iPhone was first released in the United States on June 29, 2007. Ten years ago, many of us owned a smartphone, and if we could do almost everything that we can do today via digital devices (the iPad was released in April 2010), most of us did not.

The digital devices were available; however, they were not as pervasive, and certainly not ubiquitous. Most of the companies – Google, Spotify, Netflix, Airbnb, Uber, Strava, Slack, Twitter, Facebook, LinkedIn and YouTube, to name a few – that were going to shape our everyday interactions with one another, with ourselves and with companies and services had already been founded. Certainly, entrepreneurs toyed with ideas and concepts, which are now well established; however, those concepts and ways of interaction had not yet found their spot in our everyday life. We were – at least sometimes – still buying (and using) CDs and renting DVDs. We may still have called hotels to book a room and walked (or phoned) the restaurant for a pizza. We were running without knowing exactly how many kilometres we were running and at which pace.

We Were Going Fast. . .

Through our rapid adoption of digital devices and the lagging but corollary change of behaviour, we were expeditiously increasing the pace of the digital revolution. By 2016, 3,668 billion smartphones were already circulating around the globe, and according to Statista, that figure has now doubled to a whopping 6,259 billion;[1] implying that around 84% of the world population (7.9 billion) is now digitally connected.

Now, what about our behaviour? Well, it has also evolved, as we now spend much more time in front of our screens – between 1.5 and 7 hours per day on average for the western world!

This is a cause for concern, and screen addictions are now a well-identified pathology. Consumer buying behaviour has also advanced. The 24/7 communication characteristics of mobile technology have not added or withdrawn any steps in the consumer's purchase journey; consumers still undergo the need, research, purchase, experience, and sharing of experience stages. However, with a mobile phone, which acts now as a digital extension of us, all these moments have now been merged into what some authors have described as a digital ubiquitous moment of truth (Muzellec & O'Raghallaigh, 2018).[2]

In the office, the pace of change was somehow slower. Decades of teaching and research in business schools taught us about linear value chains, setting prices through the markup and estimating the value of a company through its potential market size. All of it is relevant and valuable in the real world; however, it is often not as useful in the digital world.

We Need New Ways of Reading the Reality Surrounding Us

We need new models, tools and eyes to read the reality around us and the models behind the services we continuously use.

We can read everywhere about the parallelism between Uber and Airbnb and the flagship cases of the platform economy. We read articles that continuously pit Amazon and Apple against each other. Twitter, Facebook, Instagram and TikTok are all different faces of the same business. i.e., social networks. Spotify is the Netflix of music, and Netflix is the Spotify for movies.

Using comparison or what we already know, we tend to simplify the reality. By finding patterns, we wish to express a novel concept through another concept that we may be more familiar with. This book aims to avoid this and rather provides the reader with the right tools to examine the differences amongst all the digital services;

---

1 https://www.statista.com/statistics/330695/number-of-smartphone-users-worldwide/.
2 Muzellec, L. & O'Raghallaigh, E. (2018). Mobile Technology and Its Impact on the Consumer Decision-Making Journey. Journal of Advertising Research, 58, 12 LP–15. doi: 10.2501/JAR-2017-058.

and, more importantly, the complexity and sometimes the uniqueness of their business model, otherwise known as "the way they make money". Hence, let's have a look and spot the key differences between the business models of two companies that are often presented as very similar.

1.2 Spotify and Netflix: Spotting the Uniqueness of a Business Model

Spotify and Netflix are two of the greatest game-changers in the entertainment industry.

Spotify was founded by Daniel Ek and Martin Lorentzon in Stockholm, Sweden, in April 2006. It went live in 2009 in the UK, with the slogan and vision, "Music is for everyone". Nowadays, Spotify has more than 400 million users worldwide, garnering around 10 billion US dollars in revenues, while streaming most songs produced and delivered in the world.

Netflix has a longer history. Reed Hastings and Marc Randolph founded it in 1997 in California. In 1998, it went live with its first website, with 925 movie titles available, which were to be sent around the country in DVDs through the mail system. Nowadays, it has more than 220 million users spread across the globe, with almost 30 billion US dollars in revenues and a continuously evolving catalogue of movies, TV shows, and games.

These two companies are often told as similar stories in comparable industries. Spotify challenged and changed the music industry significantly by introducing a new revenue model along with several other changes. Netflix is considered the pioneer of the streaming platforms revolution that is changing various fields at once, from the television industry, which sees its affectionate viewers being less and less affectionate, as well as the cinema industry, which saw a new competitor/player entering in the game for theatres, producers, and the overall distribution chain.

They may look similar, but they have a few notable differences that can be illustrated through the value dimensions that underlie a business model and thus revisited in a digital business: value proposition, value architecture and value capture.

Value Proposition: What is the Clearest Benefit for Users?

Let's begin by assessing what these two companies propose to the market. Value proposition deals with the product or service offering and more broadly the definition of what the company proposes to its customers.

A very first exercise, useful to assess how a company portrays its offering to the market, is surfing the web – as not logged-in users – to assess the very first message it provides to a prospect. Spotify, following a promotion to acquire three months of premium for free, shows its mission: "Listening is everything: millions of songs and podcasts. No credit card needed".

These few words, and the short ad, tell a great deal about the company. It constitutes the initial value proposition. Spotify offers a freemium service focused on listening, and it deals with songs and podcasts. It can also be completely free to use. In other words, Spotify offers a legal way to listen to music and podcasts for free from all over the world, with millions of songs available at your disposal anytime, anywhere, with a tap.

Netflix starts off differently: "Unlimited movies, TV shows, and more. Watch anywhere. Cancel anytime". By scrolling down the page, we can find various call outs: the chance to watch it on your TV, download shows, multi-home on various devices, and a dedicated sections for kids.

Netflix is a streaming platform that aggregates various kinds of visual content and makes them available everywhere, paying a subscription fee that you can cancel anytime. We'll return to this notion soon.

The value proposition of the two companies seems similar to us as end-users when they are compared. It changes the object – from audio to video – but it offers great points of commonalities: it is everywhere, on-demand and digital.

Those value propositions may evolve over time and may be communicated differently.

"Listening is everything" is not the first claim they used. Spotify started off with a slightly different claim: "Music is for everyone". This shift in focus reveals the initial ambition of the company and its aspiration for the music industry.

In the early 2000s, the music industry was quite diverse. Those years are characterised by the legal battles of the music labels, trying to compete against the rising digital world. It began in the 90s when DVD/CD burners enabled people to duplicate CDs. This continued with digital services that enabled peers to share digital files, such as music. CDs sales dropped dramatically, and the more labels fought against these digital services by closing them down through legal actions for copyright violation, the more they popped up someplace else, always more successful. Among these services was uTorrent, one of the most famous peer-to-peer communities, which was headed for a short while in 2006 by Daniel Ek, just before he established Spotify.

Being aware of the piracy world, the founder of Spotify wished to create an environment where Music was for everyone – i.e., all types of listeners, but also all types of artists who needed to live off their art. The platform aimed to offer a model that was believed to be fairer than what it used to be.

Netflix also aimed to develop a better model for serving users and a better way of making money. Netflix challenged the model of big players, including Blockbuster. The Blockbuster model had a major flaw; essentially, it was making money in a manner that was distressing for the customers. Traditional rental companies let customers rent a DVD for 24 hours and then imposed late fees for anyone who failed to return the DVD in time. This was quite inconvenient for potential users who had to rush to watch the DVD in less than 24 hours or felt punished and stupid if they forgot to rush back to the store to return it.

Netflix erased those pains through a subscription-based service. Take the DVD, keep it as much as you wish, enjoy it, and when you are done, send it back. Customer value was at the epicentre of the business model.

In 2007, the company moved towards streaming services. Netflix proposed a prize of $1,000,000 to the first developer of a video-recommendation algorithm that could beat its own existing algorithm, Cinematch. The competitive set had evolved, and Netflix needed to beat a different set of companies, such as cable television in the US or pay-tv in Europe. Netflix's competitors included all companies that make, through various technologies, a premium selection of titles available for the customers.

The "Cancel anytime" slogan took on a completely different meaning. Have you ever tried to cancel a subscription on pay-tv? It is one of the most challenging adventures you may have in the entertainment world between letters, credit cards, and banks. Netflix doesn't want it. Cancel anytime. They subtly claim that the service is just so good that you will want to stay. You – the customer – are at the centre. The current slogan, "See what's next" is more subtle and does not refer to a specific attribute. As explained by Barry Enderwick, former Director of Marketing and Subscriber acquisition at Netflix (2001–2012):

> "See what is next" has at least three connotations: 1. Netflix is creating new content all the time (see the next big hit), 2. They're 'reinventing TV (see the next platform), 3. You can binge watch since episodic shows as they're available all at once (see the next show).

The implies the same focus on user value but different stories and communication tactics. . . yet it's probably dependent on what they do and how they do that wherein the two companies differ.

Value Architecture: How is the Value Created and Engineered Over Time?

How do those two digital players create value? What are their competences? What are their key assets? Who are their key partners? Overall, what are the mechanisms by which the products and services they offer acquire value that can be then brought to the market?

Both services are often referred to as "platforms", and as such, share some common characteristics.

Spotify changed the music industry, but it is not a music company. It is a tech company, which could possibly be a data company. It creates value by enabling parties to meet on its platforms through a match-making mechanism. In other words, Spotify matches customers' taste or listeners to specific artists who can deliver their music worldwide through the tech infrastructure built by Spotify.

Let's put it in a very straightforward way: artists cannot be suppliers. Suppliers are paid for what they supply, like vegetable producers who sell their vegetables to a restaurant, or movie producers who sell the rights to broadcast a movie for a certain amount of time to a television channel. There is no reason for the supplier to say no, if not for strategic reasons.

For Spotify, it was different. Spotify was required to convince copyright holders – primarily labels and publishers, but also distributors, performing rights organisations and artists to join the platform – they are providers who are not receiving money just for existing, but rather, they will make money if someone listens to them. In 2021, Spotify paid out $7 billion to the music industry. As for Airbnb or Uber, Spotify could be considered as a platform – a transactional one, as we will see later in the book.

Spotify creates value by setting up the architecture where listeners meet artists. This encounter is facilitated, thanks to a great ability to manage data. Spotify built a great recommendation algorithm through which it builds playlists, suggests songs and new artists, or simply lets you listen to something when an album is over. You usually like this feature so much that you hardly realise it.

And Netflix? Well, there is a huge point of contact: data. Still, it might probably be the only one. Netflix creates value exactly in the way we mentioned above while discussing a television channel. Netflix picks movies and tv shows, probably many more than a usual tv channel. This is probably the reason why it has several features that make it look like a platform. Netflix works as a curator of a great, large, wide and continuously changing schedule.

However, this is not what made it such a great company. Netflix, especially outside the States, achieved the greatest of its popularity starting from its original shows. House of Cards, their first great success, was followed by Stranger Things, La Casa de Papel, Squid Games, Bridgerton, The Witcher, Lupin, and several others.

Netflix is a tech company, but it is also a producer of movies, tv-series, and tv shows. Netflix heavily relies on data, which is used for individual recommendations. Better yet, it is used to decide which movies to produce, which series should be created and with what kind of casts, how to work on the plot to keep viewers engaged, and so on.

The two companies differ only slightly in their value delivery, which traditionally describes the choice made by the company for target market segments and distribution channels. Both have a general and wide target with an individual and family offering, which provides each member of the household the ability to achieve a personalised recommendation, thanks to data. Due to its value capture mechanism based on freemium, Spotify reaches a wider and younger base of individual users.

In terms of channels, they are both mobile apps, desktop apps, and third-party apps for almost any type of digital support, such as smart TVs and game consoles.

Value Capture: Where is the Money?

Value capture corresponds to the process through which the company capitalises on the value it has created to generate benefits for itself, generally in the form of revenue. Once again, the two cases seem very similar, since most of their revenues are derived from subscriptions, and yet, those revenues are managed very differently.

Spotify captures value from the listeners' side – who pay a subscription – or from advertisers – in case listeners enjoy the free service. At the end of 2021, Spotify had 406 million monthly active users, including 180 million premium subscribers who generated about 8.5 billion euros in premium revenue (i.e., subscription) and 226 million ad-supported (i.e., free) listeners who generated 1.2 billion in ad-supported revenue. Advertising serves as much of a value capture mechanism as a pain point that entices free users to convert to premium users.

However, that value is shared with the artists that contribute to creating the overall Spotify experience. After 30 seconds of playing a song, a new stream is counted. Each artist receives a pay-per-stream payment at a defined rate. Spotify reportedly pays out roughly 70% of what it gets to artists.

Netflix has a different value capture mechanism. It has a set of fixed and variable costs, related to the production of movies and series and the "rent" of external productions to be streamed on their service, but they do not share their revenues – originating from subscribers and licensing of certain original material – with external producers based on the views on the platform.

This quick comparison between the two cases shows how unique digital business models may be. They may indeed be very similar in terms of value proposition and delivery, as well as their user, technological and data focus. Yet all businesses are unique; in this instance, the two differ in how they create and communicate, as well as the manner in which they capture value.

This book aims to provide the readers with the right tools to analyse and spot the nuances of successful digital companies and properly assess the fundamentals of their business model. This analysis can be conducted using several tools and frameworks, which can be encapsulated within three dimensions that we labelled the Iron Triangle.

1.3 The Digital Business Model Iron Triangle

Three questions have obvious answers in a traditional business: **Who** creates value? What is the underpinning value architecture or the **shape** of the digital business? How is the **value sustained over time**? The answer to those questions is less clear for digital businesses, hence the imperative to ask them.

Who is Creating Value?

Spotify creates value-enabling transactions along with value analysis and processing a large amount of data, but listeners, artists and advertisers each play a key role in the business ecosystem. With even a single one of them absent, the others would not exist. Netflix creates value through its technology and the data originating from the end-users and the partners that create their valuable original products.

In both cases, the "network" plays a great role, but who is the network? And what are the contributions of participants (both sides) and the service provider in the creation of the value behind the digital business? Digital – as a technology – has enabled in an unprecedented way, the opportunities to engage participants – as value creators and/or recipients – in a network mode. Therefore, those who survive and grow master the power of network effects. This will be explored in the first part of the book.

How Do Digital Businesses Reshape Market Configurations?

Is it a platform? Is it a social network? Is it a marketplace? Is it a simple digital service? Digital services may look similar, but they often build on different value architectures that give birth to various outlooks of business models. Behind the similarities and the differences between Netflix and Spotify, we touch on the idea of market configurations. Digital reshapes industries, sometimes in quite disruptive ways. This will be the focus of the second part of the book, addressing different configurations of markets reshaped by digital players, namely e-commerce, social networks and sharing economy.

How is the Value Sustainably Captured over Time?

Finally, even if digital businesses are often perceived as free, or almost free, they can only survive if they have a good value capture mechanism. Hence, the sustainability of their revenue model over time must be carefully considered. Subscription can be a way, but it is not the only one. Platforms, for example, enable subsidisation, while data trading is another popular alternative. All ventures have a profit and loss statement (P&L) that seeks a good return on investments. Creating value is important; however, capturing part of this value and converting it into sustainable revenues is a necessity. This will be covered in the last part of the book, where we address different pricing models (brokerage model, subscription model, free-based business models) and their specificities in the digital arena.

These three perspectives, the who, the shapes and the sustainability, altogether represent a unicum for each digital business, a balanced equilibrium that's hard to achieve, but extremely consistent and eventually valuable once found.

This is the reason we called it the Digital Business Model "Iron Triangle" (Figure 1-A). The idea of the "iron triangle" emerges from Project Management, where the three main variables – time, cost, and quality – must be properly balanced in the planning phase and then managed throughout the project. During any project, something might happen that will try to unbalance the triangle, wherein the project manager's goal is to balance it back by working on the other variables.

We propose here the same for the digital leader: find your balance, manage the three variables to achieve the best trade-off between the who, the shape and the sustainability and work throughout your digital business growth to keep it balanced!

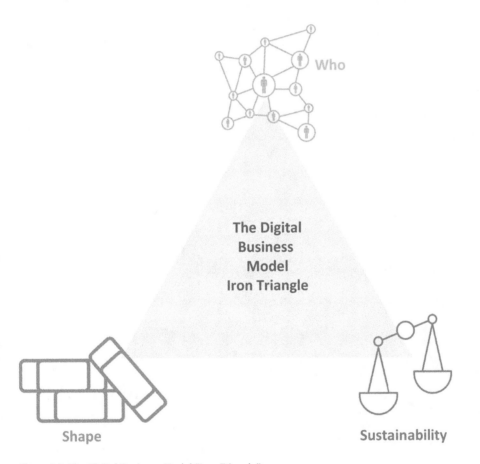

The Digital
Business
Model
Iron Triangle

Who

Shape

Sustainability

Figure 1-A: The Digital Business Model "Iron Triangle".

Part 1: Mastering the Power of Networks: Who is Creating Value?

Who

2 Looking Behind the Scene: Assessing the Value Drivers Behind Digital Business Models

As digital technology demonstrates rapid changes, it creates a highly competitive environment that forces businesses to have an effective strategy to remain relevant. The digital can be considered a catalyst for value-creation as it opens new avenues to exploit the technologies developed in the last decades. Smart devices provide a wealth of data that is yet to be fully leveraged by marketers. Behavioural data refers to information produced as a result of actions and typically tracks the sites visited, the search performed, the apps downloaded and the games played. Essentially, it allows businesses to acquire an unprecedented insight into consumer preferences at any time and any place. Yet, digital transformation no longer relies on specific technologies or activities in business. It must be consistent and coherent with the entire business. Irrespective of the industry sector (e.g., retail, services, media, advertising, travel, health, home and manufacturing), digital has become a strategic foundation of value chains and a core component of business models and value drivers.

2.1 A Digital Disruption at Work

The Impact of Digital Disruption on Business

As digital technology rapidly changes, it creates a highly competitive environment that forces businesses to achieve an effective strategy to remain relevant. Digital can be seen as a catalyst for value-creation since it opens new avenues to exploit the technologies developed in the last decades. Smart devices provide a wealth of data that is yet to be fully leveraged by marketers. Behavioural data refer to information produced due to actions and typically track the sites visited, the search performed, the apps downloaded and the games played. Essentially, it allows businesses to acquire an unprecedented insight into consumer behaviour. Marketers not only collect this data but also act on it: the mobile device is the ultimate overlapping device between the outside world and the consumers' brains. Successful corporations can populate a smartphone with relevant apps and media content that can help in capturing the location, behaviours, thoughts, mood and social network of potential or actual consumers.

Disruption is a word often associated with digital business, with a significant impact on traditional industries. Uber, for instance, although founded only in 2009, is now the world's largest taxi firm. However, unlike traditional cab companies whose fleets are generally specific to a town or city, Uber is present in more than 900 cities worldwide and owns no taxis itself. In the accommodation space, Airbnb is the biggest player. Within a decade of its inception in 2007, it is now the world's largest accommodation service provider. Although it does not own any real estate, it lists more accommodation on its website than the Hilton and Marriott chains have rooms in their hotels even after decades of doing business.

The telecommunications industry has similarly been disrupted by apps like Skype, WhatsApp and WeChat that let customers make free calls to anyone, anywhere. By using others' telecom infrastructure rather than their own, they have effectively become the world's largest phone companies. In effect, they have commoditised rather than replaced traditional telecommunications companies by turning them into mere infrastructure providers. In the e-commerce space, Alibaba has grown to become the biggest player by brokering leads between buyers and sellers on an enormous scale, although perhaps since it has no inventory of its own, it is better considered a marketplace.

Amongst media organisations, the focus for many years has been on putting digitised content on their websites. However, in recent years, social networks have revolutionised the industry by changing the way people access news. Facebook and Twitter, for instance, are now the primary news source for many, even though they do not create any news content. Currently, rather than reading articles in newspapers, people prefer getting the latest updates based on their areas of interest from specialist journalists on Twitter. The limited characters in a tweet may not allow in-depth exploration; however, it is sufficient to cover core facts and provide real-time information without waiting for news to move through the standard editorial process. The impact of digital on the print media may be assessed by the establishing outlets ceasing their print versions across the globe, for instance, *The Independent* in the UK (2016), *Wall Street Journal* in Europe and Asia (2017), *The Times Ireland* (2019) and the *Playboy* (2020) being the latest.

Netflix is the world's largest movie house but owns no cinemas. Instead, it has disrupted traditional television stations by offering a catalogue of on-demand television series, making pay-per-view movies of traditional cable television networks virtually obsolete in the process. Netflix pays to license content, after which the cost-per-view is minimal.

The largest software vendors, Google and Apple, do not write their applications but provide developers with programming tools that they can use to create applications that will run Android and iOS, respectively. This has been a huge shift in the way software is created and distributed. Rather than coding, the main challenge for Google and Apple is to maintain control over the apps in their stores that are created by third parties and to avoid those that might not share their vision or may act maliciously. In order to prevent this, both companies have an approval process for all apps.

Tomorrow's Leaders in Digital Disruption

GAMA (Google, Apple, Meta, Amazon) may also face future disruption as new companies might challenge their content, processes, and monetisation. However, they are at an advantage since they have the money to combat attacks from future competitors. For instance, they may simply buy them before they become too disruptive. An example of such a scenario is the acquisition of WhatsApp and Instagram by Facebook (i.e., Meta).

Another advantage is GAMA's status as the supplier of the digital infrastructure that is used by disruptors. For example, a cloud storage company, like Dropbox, could be using Amazon Web Services servers. Moreover, a site that offers users a quick and convenient login process might be dependent on "Facebook Connect". This means that disrupting GAMA may be risky for potential disrupters who might lose access to infrastructure, leading to a reduction in the disruptive power of such companies.

Other new players in digital business are NATU (Netflix, Airbnb, Tesla, Uber). Despite some operational (Tesla production system), regulatory (Airbnb and Uber), and competitive pressure (Netflix), these companies are registering consistent growth.

Digital Technology, Consumers' Behaviours, and Social Norms

Digital technology is also evolving the way we behave as consumers. Some companies are quicker to take advantage of those changes and define new ways of creating value. The sharing economy, for example, describes a new economic system wherein assets or services are shared between private individuals. Consumers are shifting away from fixed ownership towards a system of shared access. Instead of prioritising buying expensive items, such as houses and cars, consumers, and in particular millennials, are generally focused on the experience of collective use of resources. This usage has been enhanced by the Internet.

Eventually, technology allows for the emergence of new business models that are fundamentally changing society, sometimes by redefining our concept of social norms, for example (e.g., Facebook) or trust (e.g., BlaBlacar). For instance, in 2010, Mark Zuckerberg announced that the rise of social networking online meant that people no longer expect privacy. This assertion was conveniently aligned with the business model of the social network, which turned out to be at least partially incorrect. Yet, no one can deny that our attitudes and actual behaviour with regard to privacy have dramatically changed over the last two decades. This has been activated or at the very least facilitated by digital technology (smartphone) and the rise of social networks. Another dramatic shift in social norms can be illustrated by the users of BlaBlaCar – the world's leading carpooling company. A study by Arun Sundararajan of NYU Stern Business School showed that users of BlaBlaCar trust its drivers more than they trust their next-door neighbours. This is thanks to the trust mechanism put in place by the company. It allows users to witness the reviews from other BlaBlaCar users, creating a sense of security that brings peace of mind with respect to getting into a car with an otherwise stranger. This also exemplifies a significant shift in social norms instigated by technology.

Yet, digital transformation no longer relies on specific technologies or activities in business. It must be consistent and coherent with the entire business. Irrespective of the industry sector (e.g., retail, services, media, advertising, travel, health, home, and manufacturing), digital has become a strategic foundation of value chains.

2.2 Business Models as the Perfect Layer

Business Model: A Powerful Concept Beyond a Buzzword

"Business model" is a ubiquitous buzz phrase that proliferated largely from the internet boom of the 1990s. In the past, the term was often invoked, as writer Michael Lewis put it, "to glorify all manner of half-baked plans". Indeed, some of the early digital start-ups were not underpinned by any effective business model at all with no generation of stable and visible pricing mechanisms. Instead, such ventures often relied on flawed, advertising-driven revenue streams, and offered free value to their users. The burst of the dot-com bubble in 2001 exposed their limitations. While we may now find it easier to recognise a terrible or even an outstanding business model, many of us still struggle to define the term precisely. In its simplest form, a business model is a process which enables a company to make money. This would be an excellent definition were it not for the fact that it fails to convey the complexity of the methods used to achieve this seemingly simple goal.

Therefore, we provide a single-dimensional expression, rather than a definition, revolving solely around revenue. As Peter Drucker observed, "any definition of a business model should encapsulate all the 'assumptions about what a company gets paid for."[1] These assumptions may revolve around strategy, transaction, and particularly the notion of value. Certainly, the most widely accepted characterisation of business models is that they describe the rationale of how an organisation creates, delivers, and captures value. In this section, we first explore the notion of "value" around which the digital business models usually pivot. We then briefly outline the complementary strategic and transactional definitions of the business model.

A Value-Driven Approach to Business Model

Value is a useful concept widely utilised in economics and marketing since it measures the benefits gained by consumers from using a good or service as well as the

---

1 Magretta, J. (2002). Why Business Models Matter. Harvard Business Review, 80(5), 86–92. Quoting Drucker, P. F. (1994). The Theory of the Business. Alfred P. Sloan: Critical Evaluations in Business and Management, 2, 258–282.

benefits gained by businesses from selling the said service. In marketing, value refers to the customer-perceived value, which is the difference between a prospective customer's evaluation of the benefits and costs of one product when compared with others. In economics and for businesses, monetary worth is assigned to the technical, economic, service and social benefits a customer company receives in exchange for the price it pays for a market offering.

It is worth noting that in marketing, value is not solely derived from utilitarian benefits but also the social and emotional experience of a service. Price may affect the perception of value ("this is good value for money"), and therefore, the customer's willingness to pay; however, the price may never be equated with value. The pricing mechanism simply enhances or inhibits the acceptance of a value proposition (product and services). Prices must be consistent with the customer experience. Similarly, value does not equal revenue. Therefore, value is a fluid benefit created by the company for the benefit of consumers and the company.

Following this approach, a key question for a business remains. How can we create, deliver and capture value for and from our consumers? A business model describes the rationale of how an organisation creates, delivers, and captures value. Based on Osterwalder and Pigneur (2010), three key processes must be in place for a (digital) business to be viable (Figure 2-A):

– *Value creation:* the production of value or benefit for its consumers by the company. For instance, Google creates value for its end users by providing relevant search results.
– *Value delivery:* the governance and structure that underpins a business and which enables it to efficiently create and distribute goods and services to set standards, i.e., cost, time, quality and quantity.
– *Value capture:* the monetisation of the business through its transactions with customers for instance via payments, subscriptions, fees and/or data.

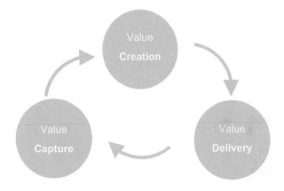

Figure 2-A: Value-driven approach of a Business Model.

Transactional Approach to Business Model

Business models, more so digital ones, may also be defined from a transactional viewpoint wherein businesses and consumers exchange value (e.g., goods, services for money, or data). In this conception of the business model, we must consider three aspects – content, structure, and governance (Figure 2-B).

– *Content:* the goods, service, or information exchanged, including the resources and capabilities required to enable that exchange. The reader may note that exchanging "content" can imply more things than simply exchanging physical goods. For instance, Facebook provides a social media platform to users at no monetary cost but only does so in exchange for users' information.

– *Structure:* the order in which exchanges take place as well as the mechanisms that enable these exchanges to occur. The structure has huge implications for the business model, especially in the digital context. This can be illustrated with Booking.com. When travellers book a room through Booking.com, they receive a confirmation email. The hotels receive a reservation notice, but not the guest's contact information. This limits their ability to employ digital marketing tactics, such as email remarketing. This structure influences the hotel industry as it limits hotel chains' marketing capabilities. However, from the perspective of Booking.com, it creates a competitive advantage.

– *Governance:* the ways in which flows of information, resources, and goods are controlled by relevant parties. This covers the organisation's legal form and how people are incentivised to transact. Hosts who post lodgings on Airbnb, for example, can "multi-home" by using other platforms to increase their occupancy rate as Airbnb does not demand exclusivity. However, the network effects associated with Airbnb ensure that it remains the first choice of the hosts despite the possibility of multi-homing.

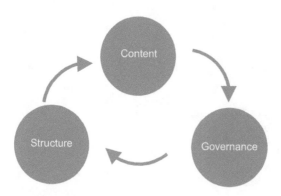

Figure 2-B: A Transactional Approach to Business Models.

Irrespective of the approach one takes to understand and explain a business model, the digital revolution has a large impact on how a business operates and creates value for its stakeholders.

In the last 25 years, new companies have emerged, and the terminology GAMAM (Google, Amazon, Meta, Apple and Microsoft) encapsulates their economic and societal predominance. More agile than older traditional companies, they quickly rose to the top, and in 2020, their market capitalisation placed them in the top five most valuable companies in the world. Today, the most valuable company in the world is Microsoft, which is valued at $1.2 trillion. With the special case of Apple, which was effectively reset as a digital company after it almost went bust in 1997, Microsoft is the only traditional business that has made its way to the top by successfully transitioning to digital.

In the 1990s, customers of Microsoft, one of the world's best-known IT companies, were required to visit bricks-and-mortar retail shops in order to buy physical copies of its Office suite that came in a box with a CD inside. However, in recent years, Microsoft has changed its model to software-as-a-service. Therefore, rather than buying a physical copy of a Microsoft product, customers now must subscribe to Office 365 for a monthly or annual fee for which they receive software updates and upgrades. Microsoft's business model evolved from traditional to digital.

Microsoft also illustrates another prevailing trend by designing a business model that locks in customers. For instance, the Seattle-based firm provides university students free access to its Office product suite, who then get accustomed to using software such as PowerPoint and Word. This makes them much more likely to become subscription-paying users following their degrees. Since they have grown used to the "Microsoft user experience", they are less likely to switch to other products when they continue with their career after graduation. Of course, Microsoft's transformation is much greater than the Office 365 example, which is almost anecdotal in comparison to other aspects of its transformation. Microsoft's digital transformation is rooted in a cultural shift initiated by Satya Nadella in 2014. It took the form of massive investments in future technology, such as cloud and Artificial Intelligence (AI). In 2017, Microsoft launched an AI division with more than 5,000 computer scientists and software engineers. It also launched Intelligent Cloud, which included products such as Server and Azure. However, the Office 365 example illustrates how technology may have a profound impact on the way companies create, deliver and capture value. The move from software as a product to software as services hereby described is much more than a simple change of distribution tactics (value delivery). Combined with a new billing strategy (value capture), it illustrates an evolution of the business model.

2.3 Value Drivers Behind Digital Business Models

At the Root of e-Businesses

The drivers of value creation outlined by Amit and Zott (2001)[2] are still applicable for digital business models today. The two authors explore how value is created in e-business by examining 59 American and European e-businesses. They observed that e-businesses create value through four interdependent drivers, namely efficiency, complementarities, lock-in and novelty (Figure 2-C). These dimensions may be illustrated using the example of Google.

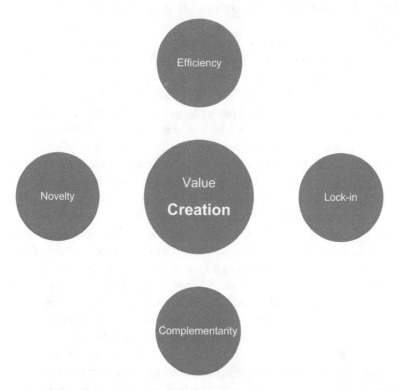

Figure 2-C: Value Drivers Behind e-Businesses.
(Adapted from Amit & Zott, 2001)

When Google first introduced its search service, end users were quick to adopt it, usually for its efficiency. Google's page-rank algorithm was a closer match to users' requirement than the existing practice of ranking the page based on category and/or

---

2 Amit, R. & Zott, C. (2001). Value Creation in e-Business. Strategic Management Journal, 22(6–7), 493–520.

money received (e.g., Yahoo!). Another novel factor for the users was a clean user interface, which incorporates only a search box to "google" a query. Due to the relevance, reliability and speed of its search results, Google became synonymous with an online search. Google use is likely to be frequent as users continue to find the relevant results that they are looking for, thereby creating a mental lock-in effect, therefore becoming a goal-activated automated behaviour (Murray & Häubl, 2007).[3]

The choice architecture of the Chrome browser sustains and strengthens the lock-in effect by providing the default choice of Google search by allowing the facility of directly typing the search term in the address bar. Along with the automatic login via a Gmail address, it also allows Google to collect individual behavioural data that are then integrated into the algorithm for specific, individually tailored search results. Moreover, the entire product suite offered by the company (search, e-mail, location-based services, smartphone operating systems) introduces complementarity, thus boosting the value proposition for the customers.

Data at the Epicentre of Value Creation for Digital Business

Digital technologies have drastically enhanced the volume and nature of content exchanged. It is the creation, the capture, the exchange and the exploitation of this content, which is now referred to as data that confers the value of a digital business. Digital removes frictions and provides a set of contents along the user/customer journey while harvesting the data generated by users' behaviour (browsing behaviour, location, search queries, devices, etc.).

When a customer purchases a product on their favourite e-commerce website or app, they simply exchange money for a product. The exchange remains a physical transaction, which will transit from an external supplier to a customer. Yet, the value creation process does not stop them. The consumer journey leaves a digital footprint, which will be analysed by the e-commerce platform owner to better understand the customer, their shopping preferences, and the way in which they navigate the app, along with the device they are using. This data or the aggregated data of multiple users can then be leveraged to create more value for the platform, the supplier, third parties or advertisers. In addition, traditional linear business models flow the value along value chains from suppliers to consumers. However, digital removes barriers and eases the process to transform traditional customers into producers. Typically, buyers on the e-commerce website become suppliers of content when they are enticed to produce a review/refer a friend or share their purchase on social networks.

---

3 See Murray, K. B. & Häubl, G. (2007). Explaining Cognitive Lock-In: The Role of Skill-Based Habits of Use in Consumer Choice. Journal of Consumer Research, 34(1), 77–88.

Data, therefore, takes an important dimension in the strategy and management of digital players. The **efficiency** of their processes relies on removing any frictions from the exchange activity. Data are exploited to identify **complementary** products and services by interlinking more and more players between them ("customers who liked this also liked that").

Data also reveal new ways to deliver products as well as **new** services enhanced by innovative technology development. Data are exploited to **lock** customers **in** a user experience and develop loyalty. Producing data is a relatively low-cost exercise for digital players and does not require any effort on the side of the users. Metadata capture the behavioural response and digital footprint of users as they browse through a website and carry on with their purchasing journey.

However, making sense of big data and generating insights has become a new fundamental strategic activity in those organisations. Very often, it is the main competitive advantage of digital players. It is well documented that Blockbuster's online video services copied Netflix ergonomics. Yet, despite a better catalogue of films at the time, Blockbuster failed to beat Netflix, whose algorithm and clever use of subscribers' data proved to be an unbeatable competitive advantage.

A Change in the Structure of Transactions

As digital enhance the disintermediation and reintermediation of traditional industries and markets, it is possible to rearrange all kind of structure for the exchanges beyond the traditional Business-to-Consumer (B2C) settings:

– Consumer-to-consumer (C2C) – The fastest growing type of business model. Airbnb, BlaBlaCar and Tinder are some examples of disintermediation of traditional exchanges before being powered by central players concentrating assets to deliver a standardised value.

– Consumer-to-business (C2B) – Businesses using digital platforms to crowdsource ideas. Lego is an excellent example where the company uses its platform to generate new ideas from Lego enthusiasts. The Irish online peer-to-peer lending platform Flender, described as a "friendly crowd finance" company, allows individuals to lend to small and medium-sized businesses. These are examples of intermediations reinvented by new participants involved and becoming active producers of the contents they would like to consume or active contributors for established businesses.

– Consumer-to-administration – Consumers starting online petitions to send to governments and political representatives through platforms such as Petition.org or Change.org is an example that demonstrates new ways to perform and act democracy that do not exist without unexpected consequences on the stability and disruption of traditional institutions.

- Business-to-administration – Digital removes traditional geographical barriers. As digital players scale, they become more global. However, in opposition, regulations remain continental (regional) or even local. Accordingly, businesses must conform their activities to local authorities and regulations regarding the exploitation of data (GDPR), taxes regulations, HR regulations, and conformity for products and services. Accordingly, they are asked to open their books with regulators and local authorities to comply with regulations. However, government agencies can save money by turning to cloud computing options that do not require purchasing costly servers and equipment. E-procurement portal over cloud is a suitable example.
- Administration-to-consumer (A2C) – Government organisations providing access to public services through online platforms. Majority of the governments in the Western world are providing such services via their citizen portals.
- Administration-to-business – The fast adoption of digital in business processes pushed administrations to adapt themselves and develop new ways to interconnect with businesses and release frictions of administrative declarations. Similar to A2C, businesses access government services online to register for new business licenses or pay their taxes. In this vein, some states are more advanced than the others and experiment a digital revolution of their processes and practices. Estonia is considered as the most advanced country in the Worlds for digitisation of administrative practices, including internal and interconnections with economic institutions and citizens.
- Administration-to-administration – State and local government organisations sharing their information systems data via data sharing protocols or open data. Administrations adapt themselves to more efficient and open processes and practices, thanks to digital adoption.

These new settings reveal new strategic priorities to govern the flow of information, resources and goods (Amit & Zott, 2001). The control of intermediations and structures by relevant parties becomes the new strategic game at play. This ecosystem uncovers the participants who will be able to sustain and develop competitive advantages throughout their journey. In this movement, the GAMAM control much of the game. These companies were not necessarily considered pioneers in their industries; however, they were able to establish large ecosystems wherein businesses, consumers and administration were required to plug their activities as a matter of efficiency. The GAMAM have quickly developed architectures to connect with users, irrespective of their location. At the heart of these GAMAMs ecosystems, we find core assets to control and govern relations among parties: tech infrastructures and continuous innovation; data concentration and exploitation; global and efficient value chains interlinking different industries; a capacity to deploy and establish new standards of user experience.

2.4 Key Takeaways and Further Considerations

Industry Trends due to Digitisation

Digitisation offers a huge potential for companies and industries far beyond the established digital players. Users and/or data are at the heart of a business ecosystem that will continue to be profoundly transformed by digital technology.

– Future Digital Opportunities for Traditional Industries and Start-Ups

While it may seem that businesses are already reaping the benefits of digital technology, McKinsey Global Institute (MGI) estimates that an additional €12 trillion may be added to Global GDP by the year 2030. MGI also predicts that AI and robotic process automation (RPA) will become the main driver of this growth. While manufacturing is slowly gearing up to tap the potential of RPA, traditional sectors, such as agriculture or retail, have started to explore AI applications. In most industries, digital start-ups now form a sizable chunk that is increasing with time. Relative to the traditional players, these start-ups are digital natives that offer value propositions derived from digital technologies. For instance, the start-ups related to speech recognition or image processing are hugely sought after by big firms such as Amazon or Microsoft.

– Further Transformation of Business Ecosystem

Digital technologies will continue to facilitate the migration of players towards areas beyond their original playground. MGI reports that digital leaders are expanding beyond their traditional industries. For instance, Amazon, starting as an online retailer, is now one of the largest providers of cloud-based services, competing directly with established technology players, such as Microsoft and IBM.

Irrespective of the sector, participating in the platform ecosystem is becoming crucial for modern businesses. For instance, sellers need to be on Amazon (or Alibaba in China) if they wish to expand their market.

While digital channels may partially hamper the growth of traditional channels, businesses need to digitise to stay relevant. Moreover, the dynamic digital landscape requires that businesses continuously innovate their product and services. Lego is an excellent example; the company has only diversified its traditional offerings and optimised its production and delivery process, thanks to digital technology. It is also harvesting the creativity of its community to crowdsource ideas for new Lego sets via a dedicated platform at ideas.lego.com.

– Investment in digital capabilities but management and processes remain key to successful transformation.

To remain competitive and relevant, businesses must be at the forefront of digital technologies. Thinking beyond current trends, firms must assess the potential of and invest in emerging technologies, such as blockchain, internet of things, and/or quantum computing. For example, Google and IBM are investing heavily in building a quantum computer. Traditional companies, such as LVMH, are also acquiring start-ups around e-commerce, blockchain, AI, data analytics or natural language processing. Digital leadership and effective management of digitisation remain the key success factor for companies. Experience suggests that solely the acquisition of technology is inadequate since it requires business process reengineering and change management know-how to succeed.

More Disruption on its Way?

The COVID-19 pandemic and the corollary decision of confinement have acted as an accelerator of an existing transformation. Similar to the virus that affects the old and sick, social distancing is destroying many of the old traditional businesses (e.g., cinema and restaurants). However, it is boosting digital platforms such as Netflix, Deliveroo, Shipt, Buymie and Amazon Fresh as well as companies that help companies in their digital transformation from Microsoft to Facebook.

Other industries seem now more than ripe for disruption. Education has been majorly disrupted by the COVID-19 pandemic. Coursera, a leader in e-learning platforms, recently launched an online MBA in a partnership wherein the University of Illinois created content and then used Coursera's infrastructure to offer this programme at a lower cost than other universities' MBAs. Data from the platform can also be used to adjust and improve the course as well as provide feedback on individual students' competencies and performance, which they may use to support their job applications. On completion of the course, graduates become alumni of both Coursera and the University of Illinois. Although this partnership will raise the university's profile in the short term by making a premium course continuously available, in the long run, it is Coursera that is more likely to benefit. The trend is expected to see most universities offer online or blended degrees in the wake of social distancing measures introduced during the COVID-19 pandemic. Differentiation may be challenging for most universities, and further consolidation may be expected.

While considering future digital business models and potential disruptors to GAMAM and NATU, it is judicious to assess Asia and Africa, where conglomerates, not well known in North America or Europe, are on the rise.

Alibaba, with its mix of services and features, is a hybrid of Amazon, eBay, and PayPal. Other examples include Tencent and Xiaomi. All of these are Chinese companies whose growth has been aided by the country's large population. India is another nation that is likely to reshape digital business worldwide. For instance, India's educational platform, Byju's, has set an eye on international expansion following its huge domestic success.

In Africa, digital businesses are also creating innovative technological solutions to cater for the diaspora. Therefore, e-commerce solutions have been created that help Africans settled abroad to support their family by sending home food and household goods instead of sending them money, which might not be used for its intended purpose. If an item is available in the country, the e-commerce website pays the retailer for it and then delivers it directly to the recipient.

3 Digital Platforms: Unlocking the Power of Networks

A plethora of buzzwords exists to describe various platform-based business models: marketplaces, app economy, social networks, crowdsourcing, on-demand economy and sharing economy, etc. The specificities of those business models will be discussed in the subsequent chapters. This chapter focuses on the common characteristics and dominant features of digital multi-sided platforms, introducing strategies to create network effects and solve the chicken-and-egg problem.

3.1 We are in a Platform Economy

Companies that adopted platform business models now dominate the ranking of "most valuable companies". In 2018, seven out of the ten largest companies were platform-based (Figure 3-A). In 2008, only Microsoft would have qualified as a platform business, and even this is debatable. Indeed, digital businesses are not necessarily required to be platforms. Therefore, back then, Microsoft could have been construed as a platform business with products such as Windows; however, tools such as Microsoft Office categorised it as a more traditional software-as-a-service, which is a linear way of monetising transactions through a subscription fee.

2018				2008			
Rank	Company	Founded	USBn	Rank	Company	Founded	USBn
1	Apple*	1976	890	1	PetroChina	1999	728
2	Google*	1998	768	2	Exon	1870	492
3	Microsoft*	1975	680	3	General Electic	1892	358
4	Amazon*	1994	592	4	China Mobile	1997	344
5	Facebook*	2004	545	5	ICBC	1984	336
6	Tencent*	1998	526	6	Gazprom	1989	332
7	Berkshire Hathaway	1955	496	7	Microsoft	1975	313
8	Alibaba*	1999	488	8	Shell	1907	266
9	Johnson & Johnson	1886	380	9	Sinopec	2000	257
10	JP Morgan	1871	375	10	AT&T	1885	238

*Companies based on a platform model

Figure 3-A: Most Valuable Companies 2018 vs. 2008.
(Source: Bloomberg, Google)

A large proportion of platforms are US or China-based, and none are European. Fast-growing companies, including 60% of the "unicorns", are platform-based businesses.

Today, digital platforms are an integral part of our user experience (UX). These platforms are utilised to connect with others and gain information (e.g., Facebook, Google, LinkedIn, Twitter and Instagram), purchase goods (Amazon, Alibaba and Etsy), book accommodations (Airbnb, booking.com and TripAdvisor), consume cultural goods (Spotify, Netflix and YouTube), access services on demand (Deliveroo and Uber) and load our digital devices with apps (Google Play and Apple Application Store).

Platforms revolutionise industries and organisational practices. LinkedIn, for example, not only connects professionals but also acts as an HR hub, wherein companies can post job vacancies, market their employee brands and recruit new staff. In terms of revenue, the HR hub function fetches more revenue for LinkedIn than its freemium subscription model for individuals. Google Nest creates a passive network of devices by connecting heating systems and thermostats to optimise energy consumption in our homes.

As discussed earlier, platforms act as facilitators between two or more sides at a micro-level and create value from those interactions. For the major players mentioned above, it is necessary to adopt a macro-perspective to explain their market dominance. Major platform players do not act as traditional actors in their respective industries. Usually, their dominance and ability to match any user with any supplier imply that they eventually control access to the market. They act as the ultimate intermediary between suppliers and potential users.

The market for the hotel industry is composed of mainly Internet users since a large majority of hotel rooms are booked online. Most online bookings are conducted via Online Travel Agents (OTAs) or third-party booking websites, such as Booking. com and Expedia, which offer travellers an easy-to-search database. According to PhoCusWright data from 2018, OTAs accounted for 51% of US hotel and lodging online gross bookings. According to Apptopia, Booking.com had more than 41 million downloads and 14.5 million average monthly active users, which can be easily classified as a vast market reach. On the producer/supply side, Airbnb and Booking.com can each boast more than 5 million reported listings of hotels and/or private accommodations.

Third-party bookings websites and app giants have placed themselves at the top of a market in which they do not directly take part. Neither Airbnb and Bookings.com nor Expedia own properties. Yet, they are amongst the largest short-term rental providers in the world. These apps are, in fact, giant, algorithmic, matchmaking, user-friendly and ultimate intermediaries that have displaced an entire sector to the position of a commodity supplier. Third-party booking websites are intermediaries that control access to more than 50% of the market. Hence, traditional bricks-and-mortar hotel chains, as well as independent boutique hotels, have all been displaced. They may access the market consisting of the internet/mobile phone users but only if they accept to become commodity suppliers on such platforms (e.g., provide "a place to stay" in a specific location). This enables them to compete with private homeowners for prices and reviews on those platforms since hotels do not enjoy direct digital access to the market.

We can illustrate this further at the micro-level of an individual user. When in need of a place to stay, users may initially search Google. For example, a search on Google with the keyword "Hotel in Dublin" returns top paid results (ad at the top) for Booking.com and organic results from Booking.com, Expedia, trivago, last-minute, Hotels.com, and KAYAK. None of them owns any hotel; however, all of them combined are able to control the access to supply (hotels in Dublin) and, reciprocally, the demand (or market) – i.e., the millions of individual internet users looking for a hotel room online. Eventually, internet users may skip the Google stage and directly perform the same search on booking.com or any of the other platforms. Either way, the result is the same for hotels – i.e., for the suppliers, in order to survive and attract potential internet users, they must accept the conditions of the platforms (a 15% commission in the case of booking.com) and compete on prices and ratings head-on with all the other room suppliers for a specific location.

However, the success of digital platforms may also inspire traditional businesses. Traditional businesses are increasingly aware of the potential of platform-based models, especially when required to compete against digital rivals. Therefore, a traditional hotel chain battling with Airbnb for holiday rentals might benefit from becoming a platform that offers conference organisation services or rents out unoccupied rooms as co-working spaces. They may also contract local providers, such as dry cleaners, to provide additional services in their hotels or offer these to nearby businesses. Although there is potential for traditional businesses to become platforms, unlike a digital business, there are considerably fewer opportunities for them to scale, since their physical location limits expansion.

So, What Are Platforms?

Platforms are not exclusive to digital businesses as they also exist in the traditional commercial landscape, although less frequently. Examples include recruitment agencies connecting employers with suitable candidates; auction houses connecting buyers and sellers of antiques and collectables; or the media industry where broadcasters serve as platforms for content producers, advertisers, and consumers.

Traditionally, goods and services were delivered from A to B through a "pipeline" approach. Companies with specific assets and competencies create value by transforming products or services. This customary method was initially described by Porter (1985) in *Competitive Advantage: Creating and Sustaining Superior Performance*. The process can be summarised in three steps (Figure 3-B). A company adds value through its supply chain management activities (inbound logistics), the transformation of material/products acquired from suppliers (operations), and finally, its distribution (outbound logistics), marketing, and customer services activities are performed.

The "platform" concept in strategy refers to a more complex and open configuration where conditions to create, deliver and capture value are not standardised

Figure 3-B: Value Chain of Traditional Businesses.
(Adapted from Porter, 1985).

and where value is created and exchanged through interactions between multiple stockholders.

Digital technology has profoundly lowered the barriers to transactions among a variety of participants by abolishing the need for physical assets. A digital platform business model creates value by facilitating exchanges between two or more inter-dependent groups (Figure 3-C), usually consumers and producers.

Figure 3-C: Value Chain of Two-Sided Digital Platform.

Sangeet Paul Choudary on the Tech blog "Platform Thinking Lab" defines a plat-form as:

> A plug-and-play business model that allows multiple participants (producers and consumers) to connect to it, interact with each other, and create and exchange value.

The goal of a platform is to propose approaches to remove the friction in the process of connecting two external but interlinked sides, typically providers/producers and users/consumers. Therefore, digital platforms often serve as UX specialists. The ease of adopting ("plug") and using ("play") is instrumental to the success of the plat-forms, particularly on the user side. The ability to connect the producers to the right consumers in a trusted environment and vice versa through algorithmic match-making capabilities is also a key feature of digital platforms.

For example, at Uber, technology acts as an "invisible hand" linking drivers with potential passengers. By sharing the location of each cab, providing an easy and secure payment mechanism, and publishing onsite reviews, trustworthy bonds are built amongst all stakeholders. Therefore, Uber becomes the custodian of that trusted connection and continuously monitors service quality.

Additionally, digital platforms can generate connectors as incentives for more than two sides to be connected. For example, the App Economy and Google Play Business Model serve as multi-sided platforms (MSPs): consumers buy devices (smartphones and tablets) that run an operating system (Android OS), which allows third-party developers to develop and present their applications on a store (Google Play). Accordingly, it acts as an MSP where the Google Play technology infrastructure is supported by the Google Play Business Model acting as a plug-and-play between end customers, editors and manufacturers, and for which Google Play must define and settle conditions to deliver a specific bundle of value propositions and ease and remove the friction in their interactions.

One of the key differences between physical and digital platforms is the simpler and cheaper conditions for scaling. A business model may be termed scalable if it is capable of coping with growth and dissociates revenues from cost-to-serve – i.e., when it can maintain its fixed costs while revenue grows in proportion to the number of new customers.

For example, it only took Airbnb four years to amass 650,000 rooms around the world (in 192 countries). However, Marriott – a traditional player in the hotel industry – took around 90 years to record 697,000 rooms in 80 countries. This demonstrates that the platform-based model of Airbnb scaled much more rapidly. Although both companies are part of the same accommodation industry, they occupy very different places in the industry eco-system.

> Platform-based businesses have radically disrupted the traditional business landscape. Not only by displacing some of the world's biggest firms, but also by transforming familiar business processes, consumer behaviour and value creation, and altering the structure of major industries. (Peter Fisk, 2019, on his personal website)

The Network Effects Behind Platforms

Enhancing interactions between (at least) two independent but interlinked sides (producers and consumers) relies on tapping into the benefits of the so-called *network effects* (Figure 3-D).

To enable these exchanges, platforms harness and create large, scalable networks of users and resources accessible on demand. Platforms develop communities and markets with network features, which allow users to interact and transact.

Network effects have previously been observed in non-digital contexts. For example, it is not worth owning a phone if none of your friends and connections do. The value of a phone increases dramatically as more and more of your friends own one.

Similarly, the more participants (peers) on Skype, Facebook or WhatsApp, the more valuable it is for any potential user to join a social network platform. A *same-side network effect* occurs when the value of a product or service grows according to the number of others using it. Economists name them as *direct positive network effects* (or *demand-side economies of scale*). Sometimes, the same-side network effects can be negative. For example, the more the users connect from the same location to book an Uber taxi, the lesser the cars available and the higher the price due to Uber's "Surge Pricing Strategies".

For digital platforms connecting at least two different sides, network effects may be described as *indirect network effects* (or ***cross-side network effects***) since the value of a platform for one side (consumers or producers) is based on the number of participants from the other side (consumers or producers). For example, the more sellers you have on Amazon, the more attractive it is for end customers to shop there. Reciprocally, the more the potential buyers on Amazon, the more attractive it is for sellers to join it and advertise their goods. The same reasoning can be extended to travellers and hosts on Airbnb, drivers passengers on BlaBlaCar, etc.

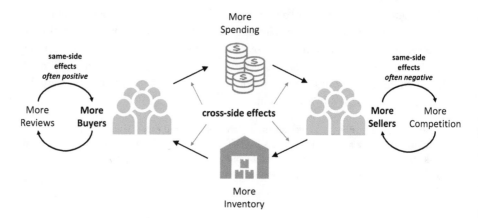

Figure 3-D: Illustration of Same-Side and Cross-Side Network Effect.

Considering platform-based business models as the rationale through which the platform-owner (also called "the matchmaker" by Evans and Schmalensee[1]) removes friction in the process of connecting, creating and exchanging value and thus enabling interactions between at least two external but interlinked sides is equivalent to mastering the network effects at work through the permitted interactions.

---

1 Evans, D. S. & Schmalensee, R. (2016). Matchmakers: The New Economics of Multisided Platforms. Harvard Business Review Press.

Information and digital technologies eliminate friction and facilitate low-cost interactions on a large scale. Mastering network effects lead to new strategic horizons. For several years, we considered that the first to enter an industry would benefit from this speed advantage in the long run and attain a monopoly position. This may not always be the case. Digital ventures demonstrate that dominant positions emerge from abilities to manage (create and extend) network effects among participants of all sides and capture part of the value generated in the process.

Network effects come into play at each layer of a platform (value creation, connection, and exchange) and at each stage of development of a platform (from ignition to maturity). As we will demonstrate, platforms and markets must satisfy some conditions, which change and differ over time and depend on the scalability of digital platforms.

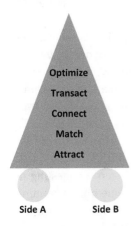

Figure 3-E: Platform Launch Rocket.
(Source: adapted from *Launchworks*)

Launchworks illustrate how companies may create network strategies using the analogy of launching a rocket (Figure 3-E). Immense energy is required to lift the rocket off the ground by attracting both sides of the market on the platform. The core jobs of the platform are then to match, connect and entice transactions between those two sides, which will interactively optimise the process of transaction development, leading to the analysis of accumulated data. Essential conditions are observed for the two sides to easily connect (plug) and begin interacting or transacting (play).

3.2 Creating Conditions for Plug and Play

Adopting a platform-based business model is difficult. Start-ups, for which the value proposition is intrinsically dependent on the participation of multiple sides, will often struggle to develop the perfect matchmaking mechanisms along the development path.

Facebook provides an interesting example of the network effects for both the same-side and cross-side. The same-side effect was evident at the foundation of Facebook. It began as a social network involving peer-to-peer connections with users creating content (posts) that were consumed by friends who read, viewed, "liked", shared or commented on. This agglomeration of family, friends and groups formed a network: the peers' side. The initial goal was to reach a critical mass of peers and end-users.

The Facebook website was launched on February 4, 2004, from a dorm room at Harvard College in Boston. At the time, sign-up was limited to Harvard students, catering to a very small and specialised market (as a proof of concept). The website was a simple online website application of a "face book", which is a directory consisting of individuals' photographs and names. Face books are traditionally distributed by some American universities – albeit at the time not in Harvard – at the start of the academic year, to help students know each other better.

Facebook, the website, became popular amongst students across several campuses and rapidly opened to the public in 2006. Henceforth, anyone 13 years or older was able to sign up for its member page. Since its beginning, it remained free for peers to log in, create and exchange with others. "Free" was a huge accelerator for adoption and a way to eradicate frictions and enhance the same-side network effects. Several factors contributed to Facebook's mastery of the network effect. The same-side effect was visible in the form of viral lifts. Friends felt peer pressure to connect to the platform to avoid becoming the only member of their group unconnected to Facebook. Facebook also employed engagement triggers, suggesting potential friends or pages to "like" based on a user's interests, something determined by an algorithm that examined how they had interacted with the platform over time. Non-pricing mechanisms were powerful enough to establish a base of about 2 billion active members by 2017.

The cross-side network effect was based on the number of users on the platform and their level of activity. Offering the service for free ensured the highest adoption rate with the launch of Facebook. The more time users spend on the platform, the more the value accrued to the advertisers; therefore, gaining a critical mass of users first was essential. By October 2007, Facebook already had 50 million active users, five times the number of users in the year before. It was only then that Facebook introduced a large-scale official ads program to the platform. Advertisers are essential to Facebook's business model since advertising revenues enable the platform to remain free for users. In turn, users accept that their data may be used commercially to present them with relevant adverts. In other words, Facebook users exchange their data as "virtual currency" to freely access Facebook.

Its 2019, Facebook's revenue accounted for $70.7 billion, of which $18.5 billion was the net income. However, it took around eight years since Facebook's inception to generate a positive net income. It was at that price to establish a dominant social network and capture value from generated network effects. Since it was free to use, it was a necessity to connect other sides to the platform to generate a sustainable business model in the end.

In order to create and nurture strong network effects, digital ventures must pay attention to the consistency of the "Five Ps" (analogous to the 4 Ps of Marketing) as outlined by Accenture[2] (2016).

Proposition

A platform should be able to offer a dedicated value proposition for each side. For instance, YouTube facilitates interactions between three key stakeholders or sides (content creators, users and advertisers). These stakeholders benefit from each other's presence while also being attracted to the platform through varying value propositions. YouTube presents a highly visible hosting platform (with an earning potential) to the content creator. It provides end users (largely) free access to unlimited content deemed relevant to them. It also offers an unmatchable reach to potential customers and advertisers.

Personalisation

A successful platform should value data and offer personalised user journeys based on customer type and usage history while respecting the privacy laws of the market. We are familiar with Netflix recommendations based on our watch history and content localisation as well as Facebook's or YouTube's specific recommendations of content according to our browsing history and digital footprint within, or even outside, the platform. These mass customisations are possible at a large scale based on cookies, users' data and metadata, which activate algorithms to conjure the feeling of a personalised experience. These tailored experiences increase the participants' willingness to transact and ultimately lock themselves into the platform.

Pricing

Pricing mechanisms remain significant as they condition the value captured by the platform owner and can enhance or inhibit friction to connect, create, and transact. Smart platforms make use of dynamic pricing based on user characteristics, product/service experience and market context.

A large majority of transaction platforms prefer to charge a small fee on each transaction to capture the value permitted by the platform. These pricing mechanisms

---

2 Accenture Report. (2016). "Five ways to win with digital platforms".

directly flow from the ease of interactions; however, the transaction fee characteristics can vary according to the structure and governance of exchanges. For example, Airbnb eases the booking of a stay for a specific period, but each transaction is different (traveller, host, period and product characteristics). Since the traveller will experience the goods later, Airbnb secures the conditions of the transaction by collecting the payment from the traveller and releasing the payment to the host 24 hours after the beginning of the stay. Airbnb charges fees on both sides: service fees on the "travellers' side" that varies across countries according to local taxes and fees on the "host side" that are justified by the transaction enhanced (as a real estate agent) and the security on payments. Hosts are free to determine the price of their rentals according to seasonality and personal considerations; however, Airbnb makes use of its data analytics and predicts the occupancy rates according to pricing adopted by the hosts to offer them suggestions (smart pricing). In another context, Uber adopts similar mechanisms for pricing and collecting a fee on each transaction. However, it imposes the pricing for each ride based on their algorithms. This pricing is continuously revised according to laws of demand and offer in the local area (surge pricing), which benefits Uber as well as its drivers.

Other kinds of platforms that release digital content (Netflix and Spotify) generally adopt subscription-based pricing mechanisms to transform the products-as-a-service (as we will describe in Chapter 5) and charge for network access. To ease adoption and remove frictions behind network effects, a few other services provided by a platform prefer subsidising the service for one side by another side (third-party subsidy as we will describe in Chapter 4). Examples include YouTube, Google SEO, Facebook and so on.

The pricing mechanisms are significant and require chirurgical attention to not inhibit network effects or jeopardise the sustainability of the platform owner. Platforms often struggle to fine-tune the pricing of their services and adjust it regularly.

Protection

Platforms combine a multitude of participants, propositions, and pricing mechanisms. This heterogeneity poses inherent uncertainties and challenges for interaction between participants. Hence, platforms must build strong trust mechanisms to secure participation in this ecosystem. Trust mechanisms can take the form of user authentication (e-mail, phone number, Facebook profile, etc.), payment security, a rating system of the participants or the conditions of exchange (shipping and quality of the goods). This latest feature serves as a proxy for positive word of mouth, thereby becoming essential for the sustainability of a trust-based ecosystem. It positively influences prospective users and entices future transactions.

Partners

Compared to traditional business organisations, platform-based businesses develop more pervasive architectures of value. Focused on a core set of activities and competencies on the inside, they interconnect their technological architectures with the main companies (e.g., Amazon for data storage, Google and Facebook for login and SEO, and banking APIs to ease payment proceedings). They further extend their ecosystems by interlinking their value with complementors. A smart platform builds an architecture that allows it to interact with each partner in a smooth manner.

3.3 Platform Development Stages

Multi-sided platforms (MSPs) face different challenges at various stages of their development.

Typically, four main stages in the development of platforms can be identified, with specific strategic questions to address regarding the deployment of their business model. We will investigate each of these stages and offer some insights and key tactics to navigate along the way.

Embryonic Stage

In this stage, the founders and platform owners must focus on the design of the platform as the core product and the architecture of the service. As previously mentioned, the consistency of the 5 Ps (Proposition, Personalisation, Pricing, Protection and Partners) must be addressed with a focus on the value proposition and value architecture (core activities, technologies, and business partners). A minimum value proposition can be designed and tested with real participants. It can be a "smaller world" or a one-side service subsidising the other sides and acting as a pipeline.

At this stage, the objective is to achieve a proof of concept of the adoption of the value proposition and the unique selling proposition with the proper technology architecture to ease transactions and service, such as when Airbnb was launched only in San Francisco or when Facebook was launched as a closed service for Harvard College peers.

Emergent Stage

This stage involves the demonstration of the product-market fit, where the product is the platform. Hence, the focus shifts to the recruitment of participants on both sides (producers and consumers). This stage also debuts the first major challenge of achieving network effects, known as the "chicken-and-egg problem". It derives its name from that age-old question: "Which came first, the chicken or the egg?" Who should platform startups attract first? The producers or the consumers? This is a difficult question to answer as each is motivated by the presence of the other side.

Entrepreneurs will be required to demonstrate their ability to attract participants on both sides. Their ability to raise funds to scale and grow (next stage) is dependent on their success in this stage. The chicken and eggs and associated issues are covered in the next section of this chapter.

Growth Stage

Once the platform gains a critical mass of end-users, the focus shifts towards the monetisation and monitoring of trust and loyalty issues.

In this scaling phase, the platform must scale the number of transactions and ensure that they capture sufficient value to be sustainable and produce a return on investment for their first investors. The focus is no more on the product-market fit but the efficiency of customer-transaction fit.

Fortunately, as the business grows, the expansion accelerates and streamlines. It took Uber approximately 18 months to expand into a second country, but then only 60 days to open in the next. This occurred due to the streamlined legal and marketing process, which helped them to become faster in their establishments. However, as a business scales up, it must ensure not only that it has enough funding but also that it is continuing to build enough trust and loyalty so that customers return and competitors are repelled. It must also raise the volume of transactions. Hence, a company such as Airbnb with an average stay of $70 per night for three nights should attempt to attract more premium customers or increase the average stay length.

Monitoring customer acquisition costs and the lifetime value of the customers is crucial. The platform must become a one-stop shop for travelling (Airbnb), for shopping everything (Amazon) and searching for videos (YouTube), etc.

As the volume of transactions increases rapidly in this stage, trust issues may develop. Therefore, protection mechanisms must be reactive to avoid a backfire.

Maturity Stage

At this stage, the focus is on the optimisation of the offerings to create maximum value, embracing the maximum number of participants/sides, and diversifying the services and monetisation. Google and Facebook as well as Amazon and Apple offering various advertising tools on their platforms reflect this stage of the diversification of their offerings. The strategic focus is on defending the platform ecosystem against other giant ecosystems, and in doing so, the platform owner must act as a keystone (a value dominator) of an ecosystem where they aggregate the innovations from other complementors (by buying/authorising innovations) and defending their dominant position with the landlords (lead participants) with whom they have developed strong ties.

The main challenge at this stage is to continue to grow the business and defend its position against potential disruptors.

3.4 Facing the Chicken-and-Egg Issues

As stated earlier, platforms work once they have managed to trigger a network effect – i.e., when the value of using the platforms increases with the number of participants.

For the cross-side effect, MSPs must attract at least two mutually interdependent users. Yet, each side has an incentive to come on board once the other side exists; hence, it presents the metaphysical "chicken-and-egg question". It is a complex issue with several underlying challenges. As seen earlier with the rocket launch analogy, this ability to attract both sides (e.g., buyers and sellers) and run development and marketing for them requires significant energy.

The challenges relate to participants and the tricks to attract them. For a platform to work, both producers and consumers must be on board. Consumers act as bait to lure the producers and vice versa. This is known as the **mutual-baiting problem**. However, how do you attract buyers to a platform when you have no sellers, and how to attract sellers when you have no buyers? How do you seed the platform with users on both sides and spark interactions? At least one side of the platform should be present to act as bait for the other.

A related set of issues pertains to the level of exchanges between sides. It is called **the ghost-town problem**, similar to an old-style Western movie, wherein a cowboy rides into town and finds the streets empty. Imagine that you can attract participants, but no activity/transaction is performed. Generating trust and confidence is a major issue, and this is an indicator of low motivation to exchange and transact for participants.

Several solutions exist to overcome the challenges outlined above and reach critical mass on both sides of the platform. Here are a few tactics and strategies successfully employed by many platforms over the last 20 years.

Concentrate on Users Who Can Belong to Both Sides

One solution to overcome the mutual-baiting challenge is to target a very specific group of users who can fit on both sides of the network, such as those who could serve as both chicken and egg, depending on the time and the situation.

For example, eBay did this when it launched as a platform by focusing on attracting collectors, specifically those who collected watches and clocks as collectors' markets are composed of people who may both buy and sell such objects. It then focused on other types of collector markets, from where it flourished.

A variant of this technique that may be used at a later stage of development is known as side switching. This tactic is to incentivise users to switch sides. For example, once a user has finished the booking process on Airbnb, they are immediately incentivised to become a host. After all, the user's residence will be empty while they are travelling; hence, the value proposition is obvious: why not earn some money while you are away (to finance your vacation)? This is an amazing marketing trick since it not only solves the mutual-baiting problem, but also enhances the traveller experience and ensures that hosts deliver the best experience to travellers.

Subsidise One Side (or Even Both)

Providing bait to whichever side is the most difficult to possibly seed through price discount is one option. Seeding can also be accomplished by other techniques.

For example, dating websites work when they have a male and a female audience. Attracting males is usually not too difficult. For females, it is far more complicated. Dating websites are typical of asymmetrical markets with one side harder to attract (the "hard" side) and the other, which is relatively easier to obtain traction on (the "easy" side). To solve this issue, monetary incentives can be offered to the hard side. Similar to how nightclubs often host a weekly "Ladies Night" where women receive free entry and/or free drinks, dating websites can offer free membership and a better experience for women. This model is inherently typical of most platforms, which would have a "subsidy side" that allows the use of the platform with discounts or even for free, and a "monetary side" that is charged for participation or transactions.

Platforms may choose to go even further to attain a critical size by subsidising both sides at least until a certain point. YouTube, which was established in February 2005, allowed both viewers and content creators, including companies, to use the platform for free. However, it did not entice companies to advertise on its website before November 2009. YouTube analytics was only launched in 2011.

Similarly, Facebook also encouraged both users and companies to join the platform. Individual users enjoyed a same-side effect and were happy to communicate with each other for free. In order to attract businesses, Facebook launched fan pages in 2007; companies were initially invited to create pages to freely engage with fans. In the very early days, most fans would see the posts generated by the brand, which would not cost the fan page owner any money. Gradually, businesses started to realise the benefits associated with this emerging media. The number of businesses present on the platform grew exponentially, and so did their willingness to pay. It was time for Facebook to begin capturing the value it created. By 2012, organic reach (the % of people who see a business page post without paid distribution) had already fallen to 16% and declined further to 6.5% in 2014. Many observers believe that it is now lower than 2% on average. This means that companies almost systematically pay Facebook to reach and engage with their targeted audience.

Platform Staging

By default, platforms do not have any standalone value. Yet, to overcome the mutual baiting challenge, companies might first develop a one-sided value proposition that can be embraced without network effect. This tactic is part of a platform staging strategy. The platform may initially not serve as a double-sided market; however, it would act as a single-side service to attract the side which is most difficult to seed. OpenTable allows individual users to book a restaurant table with ease and for any occasion. To draw restaurants onboard, OpenTable first helped them to manage their booking online. It provided restaurants with an application that allowed them to manage the relationship with their customer base via their website. This facilitated the work of restaurants and was an attractive solution for restaurant owners, regardless of a network effect. Yet, the network effect was easily achieved, as once the solution was adopted, it was de facto linked to the B2C OpenTable website, where individual users of the platform could also book a table.

Similarly, the taxi-booking app, Hailo (now called FREE NOW), managed to rapidly secure the participation of most black cabs in London by initially providing only mobile payment and real-time traffic. Those essential features are valuable regardless of the participation of users on the other side of the network. The possibility of gaining new customers via the app was a bonus that quickly became the main feature of the app once adoption by passengers skyrocketed.

A variation of this strategy is to alternate or stage its communication to one side and then the other. For example, the car-sharing platform BlaBlaCar used the notorious French railway strike to recruit users. In October 2007, it used the opportunity to send a press release to "own the moment". The news of such a useful website implied that during the strike, the platform was featured in over 500 newspaper articles and received massive attention on TV and radio. Yet, during strikes, it is relatively easy for BlaBlaCar to recruit stranded passengers looking for a ride. Hence, for the subsequent (and frequent) railway strikes, BlablaCar now has solely focused its PR campaign on attracting drivers by appealing to their sense of solidarity.

Platform Envelopment

This partnering strategy relies on leveraging the shared relationships with (other) established platforms and their networks to strive and combine value propositions and benefit from a multi-platform bundle that leverages shared user relationships. For example, millions of users rapidly adopted Spotify since it was initially integrated into mobile operators' plans.

There is no "one best way" to overcome the chicken-and-egg problem. In several cases, a challenge faced by platform start-ups is to present enough choices to meet demand. As the number of choices corresponds to the number of search results on a page, if the first page of a platform search displays nine results, users will expect to see nine options. Meeting this demand is a serious challenge, particularly in the early stages. However, this is just the start of the journey for platforms. They must cultivate a long-term perspective to sustain their competitive advantage.

Table 3-A presents a set of tactics to overcome the chicken and egg dilemma.

Table 3-A: Tackling the "Chicken-and-Egg Problem".

Tactics	Definitions	Impacts On
Single Target Group e.g., Uber setting up in a specific city to replicate and scale globally after.	It consists of reducing the total market size and the required critical user mass. Fewer resources and less time are required to reach the critical inflexion point from which the MSP can grow to other market segments.	Mutual-Baiting Problem Ghost-Town Problem
Platform Staging e.g., Amazon for bestseller books, OpenTable with a B2B value proposition	It consists of evolving in two distinct steps: from a traditional vendor-based (pipeline) business model in the first stage to a platform-mediation business model in the second stage after reaching the critical user mass.	Mutual-Baiting Problem Double Company
Subsidising e.g., YouTube	It typically consists of a subsidy side that allows the use of the platform with discounts or even for free, and a monetary side that is charged for participation or transactions.	Mutual-Baiting Problem
Platform Envelopment e.g., Spotify integrated into mobile operators' plans, Internet Explorer embedded in Microsoft OS	This partnering strategy relies on leveraging the shared relationships with (other) established platforms and their networks to strive to combine value propositions and benefit from a multi-platform bundle that leverages shared user relationships.	Mutual-Baiting Problem

Table 3-A (continued)

Tactics	Definitions	Impacts On
Side Switching e.g., eBay with collectors; Airbnb where (with incentives) travellers can become hosts	This involves making a two-sided platform one-sided by finding a platform design that allows users to fill both market sides of the MSP simultaneously.	Mutual-Baiting Problem Ghost-Town Problem

(Adapted from Stummers et al., 2018).[3]

3.5 Key Takeaways and Further Considerations

1. Platforms adopt plug-and-play business models that allow multiple partici-pants to connect to them, interact with each other, and create and exchange value.
2. Platforms must act as matchmakers and master network effects that condition their existence and sustainability.
3. Platforms face several challenges at different stages and must remain agile in their developments, which requires several resources and staging development tactics.

"The Eyes Can Only See What the Mind Is Ready to Understand"

As designed by Osterwalder et al. (2014), the original Value Proposition Canvas is best suited to traditional corporations with a pipeline strategy, where producers are seated at one end and consumers at the other. However, with platforms, both pro-ducers and consumers can be customers of the business. Thus, we must adapt it to account for at least two-sided platforms.

In Figure 3-F, the adapted and revised Value Proposition Canvas demon-strates the pains and gains of producers and consumers and the distinct, non-related value propositions the company requires for each side. For instance, the value of Facebook's advertising platform originates from the gain advertisers achieve from being able to micro-target audiences. However, if consumers do not prefer targeted advertising, they will classify it as a pain. Alternatively, if they ap-preciate personalised suggestions for products on their news feed, they will con-sider this a gain.

---

3 Stummer, C., Kundisch, D., & Decker, R. (2018). Platform Launch Strategies. Business & Informa-tion Systems Engineering, 60(2), 167–173.

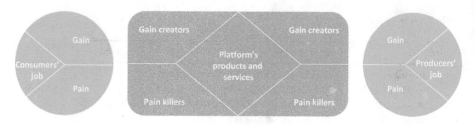

Figure 3-F: A Two-Sided Value Proposition Canvas.
(Adapted from Osterwalder et al. 2010)

Alternatively, many consulting companies presented Digital Platform Canvas as an alternative to the Value Proposition Canvas with Core Interaction at its centre (Figure 3-G). For instance, the core interaction for YouTube would be the sharing of videos with an audience, which can be enhanced by facilitators (the rules and the types of content allowed), tools and services (search engines and toolkits for uploading videos to the site), filters (keywords associated with a video) and potential partners (those who deepen the interaction through the development of applications).

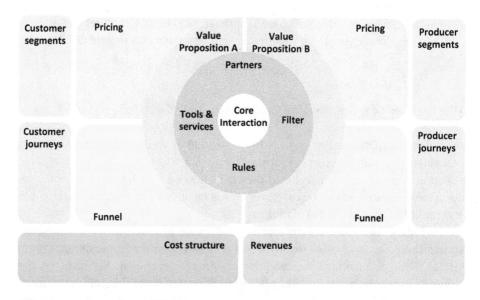

Figure 3-G: An Alternative Digital Platform Canvas.

As with other versions of the Canvas, the producer and customer are on the opposite sides, along with their respective value propositions. Since adoption is generally the key challenge for a company, traditionally, the value propositions are customer-oriented. In contrast, this Canvas accommodates journeys for customers and producers as well as the channels (funnels) and pricing for each side. Finally, cost structure and revenue are examined, which might also differ for each side. This reinvented Canvas enables companies envision key elements for both sides and helps them illustrate the value proposition for consumers and producers.

The Evolving Nature of Platforms' Value Propositions

The value proposition(s) and the business model must not be necessarily static. In fact, they should change and evolve according to value appropriation and sustainability and scale of value captured.

Many platforms fail to adjust them, resulting in stagnation. This is particularly true for traditional businesses attempting to survive in an increasingly digital business atmosphere. Nearly 90% of start-ups fail within the first five years of business, a key reason being their inability to adapt to their business model. Of those that do survive, 60% no longer operate according to their original value proposition. For instance, newspapers' primary source of revenue has always been the sale of advertising space on their pages. However, to survive and stay relevant in a world where more people seek news online, they now offer online versions and sell digital advertising space using tools such as Google Display Network. Thus, it should be considered that business models are not static, and the platforms should be willing to revise their value proposition(s) in changing circumstances.

Part 2: **Reshaping Markets: How is Value Configured?**

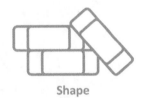

Shape

4 Marketplaces: Better, Faster, Stronger? Removing Frictions in E-commerce

It is evident for us to begin this second part with commerce and how digital reshaped configurations for business. Digital technologies enhanced the potentialities of trading and interconnecting in different ways with respect to both buyers and sellers. With that being said, we observe the emergence of a dominating model for e-commerce: marketplaces progressively replacing the traditional retailer model. What may be the reason behind this, and what are the characteristics of a business model in underlying marketplaces? Paraphrasing Daft Punk, are they better, faster and stronger?

4.1 The Rise of Digital Merchants

Modern e-commerce was kick-started with the emergence of Amazon and eBay. In 1995, Jeff Bezos launched Amazon as an e-commerce platform for books. In the same year, Pierre Omidyar launched an auction platform that would later become eBay. Four years later, Jack Ma founded Alibaba in 1999. Alibaba became profitable in 2002, with Amazon following suit the very next year.

These companies heralded an e-commerce revolution that encouraged other players to enter the fray. While online sales stood at around 5% of overall retail sales in the US in 2007, they reached 16% by the year 2019, with US consumers spending more than $600 billion online. At the global level, Grand View Research[1] (2020) estimates that the global e-commerce market stood at around $9.09 trillion in 2019, with estimated growth at a compound annual growth rate of 14.7% from 2020 to 2027.

So, What Propels the Rise of E-commerce?

At the 2011 *Fórum E-Commerce in Brazil*, eBay's Vice President of Corporate Strategy at the time, Jean-Francois Van Kerckhove, identified five key trends eBay believed would shape the future of e-commerce, namely mobile, local, global, social and digital.

While those five trends are still relevant, it is mobile technologies that have fundamentally changed the way consumers shop online. Mobile technology is an essential consideration during the creation and evolution of any e-commerce business.

---

[1] Grand View Research Report, May 2020, "E-commerce Market Size, Share & Trends Analysis Report By Model Type (B2B, B2C), By Region (North America, Europe, APAC, Latin America, Middle East & Africa), And Segment Forecasts, 2020–2027".

French e-commerce company Vente-Privee (Veepee), for example, increased sales by 20% just by developing an app for smartphones and tablets that offered a mobile-friendly user experience.

Mobile technology significantly influences e-commerce globally, often in countries that have historically experienced slower technological growth due to limitations in infrastructure and technology. In Africa and parts of Asia, for example, smartphones are popular since they overcome some of the infrastructure limitations, such as the lack of fibre optics. Mobile payment technologies have also enabled businesses to benefit by developing mobile sites that may quickly become profitable.

Mobile also connects the other factors identified by Van Kerckhove. Hence, in digital terms, it enables in-context payments. For instance, in order to continue playing a mobile phone game such as Candy Crush, consumers must make an in-app payment using a touch ID or by credit card, the details of which are stored on the device. With the launch of smartphone wallets including Apply Pay, Google Pay and AliPay, the mobile payment market is destined to grow across the world. The global mobile payment market *was* estimated[2] to be at around $1.14 trillion in 2019 and is expected to grow to about $4.7 trillion by 2025, registering a compound annual growth rate of more than 26%.

The ergonomics of mobile technology are especially important with respect to user experience, as the small size of phone screens limits the number of images that can be displayed on a single page. This means that image dimensions and resolutions must be changed to optimise them for the mobile viewer.

Mobile devices provide digital merchants with the ability to identify the location of their customers, leading to geo-targeted real-time ads. However, not everyone wishes to be tracked physically. Hence, if marketers don't want to alienate their consumers, they must keep in mind the cultural sensitivities relating to certain types of marketing. In Europe, for instance, using geolocation technologies for tracking is often considered invasive.

Amazon Go – a cashless and cashier-less retail store – epitomises the mobile and e-commerce revolution. Shoppers download an app on their smartphones that identifies them when they enter such a store. Cameras then track their movements and check the items they put in their baskets. When done, the customer simply walks out of the shop, receiving a receipt for their items through the app. This payment system is even more invisible than a one-click system.

---

2 See Mordor Intelligence Report 2021 on "mobile payments market – growth, trends, covid-19 impact, and forecasts (2022–2027)".

The Long Tail and Digital Merchants

In *Wired* (2004), and then in his book, *The Long Tail: Why the Future of Business Is Selling Less of More* (2006), journalist Chris Anderson coined one of the most important economic concepts behind e-commerce. The Long Tail concept is against the traditional retail strategy of "selling more of a small selection" of inventory. It considers that the future of business lies in selling low-popularity items (Figure 4-A). As indicated by Investopedia:[3]

> The head and long tail graph depicted by Anderson in his research represents this complete buying pattern. The concept overall suggests the U.S. economy is likely to shift from one of mass-market buying to an economy of niche buying all through the 21st century.

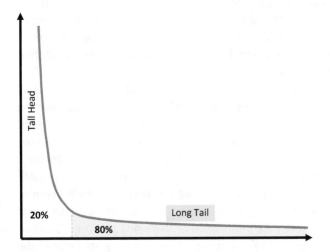

Figure 4-A: The Long Tail Economics.

In other words, "the long tail is a business strategy that allows companies to realise significant profits by selling low volumes of hard-to-find items to many customers, instead of only selling large volumes of a reduced number of popular items" (Investopedia). In order to achieve this, digital must remove the barriers and frictions for marketing and distribution costs, pushing retailers to focus on blockbusters.

As traditional physical retailers possess a limited space to display products, they are restricted in the amount of inventory they can carry in shops. This forces them to carefully select a restricted range of products that they think will sell best to local customers. Typically, this includes "blockbusters" – the most popular products at the time – such as the top 10 books on bestseller lists.

---

3 See Investopedia dedicated entry on Long Tail, consulted on May 2022.

The rationale for this is that in traditional retail shops, the Pareto principle implies that 20% of the inventory generally generates 80% of sales. Therefore, in a bookstore, J K Rowling's latest novel will entice several customers, but a niche book regarding French rugby players will not. Having fewer, low turnover non-blockbusters is also more efficient in terms of inventory management.

This is where the digital business model enters the picture. Digital merchants, such as Amazon, do not face the same limitations as physical retailers. Hence, by aggregating smaller sellers who manage the inventory for them, they can offer products that physical retailers cannot. This gives them the advantages of both long-tail and traditional retail strategies.

Pure digital retailers are at the extreme end of this continuum, and therefore, can offer a much greater array of inventory than those selling physical products. For example, a physical music shop might not be able to stock a rare recording of a 1991 Nirvana concert. However, for a pure digital retailer, it is not a problem as the inventory cost of stocking this is minimal, meaning that they can offer it alongside mainstream products, such as Lady Gaga's latest album. For pure digital retailers, the cost of offering a bestseller or a rare article is the same.

Despite such benefits, this does not imply that digital retailers do not face challenges. For instance, digital retailers have difficulties with digital rights management and contracts with record companies. Exclusivity agreements between artists, record companies and digital music providers, such as iTunes or Spotify, can become obstacles for digital retailers. Hence, a trade-off for digital merchants is always observed.

When considering e-commerce, digital merchants such as Amazon, eBay or Alibaba usually first come to mind. However, these are just part of a "digital continuum" that stretches from resellers who purchase inventory and have margins based on sales and profits at one end to pure multi-sided or two-sided platforms facilitating interactions between buyers and sellers at the other. Following are some of the main categories of such digital merchants in increasing order of their digital nature.

Business Models Behind E-retailing

As specified in Figure 4-B, we can range e-retailing business practices according to the digital nature of products and services distributed.

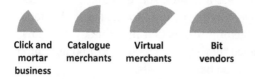

| Click and mortar business | Catalogue merchants | Virtual merchants | Bit vendors |

Figure 4-B: Continuum of eRetailing Practices Regarding the Digital Nature of Products/Services.

Click-and-mortar businesses – These are physical businesses that have become hybrid by extending their product showrooms online. Their customers either order items online for home delivery or collection at a nearby store. Such businesses often face inventory tracking and supply chain challenges due to the separation between their physical and online systems. Barnes and Noble is a classic example of such challenges.

Starting as a bricks-and-mortar business, the bookstore chain Barnes and Noble began selling through a website that was completely disconnected from its physical shops. However, salespeople had difficulty explaining to customers wanting to return an item they had purchased online why they could not do so in-store. To remove this source of frustration, Barnes and Noble merged their supply chain so customers could return online purchases in-store. This required the resolution of complicated internal issues to synchronise accounting systems between online and physical retail outlets. Following this initiative, customer service improved greatly.

Catalogue merchants – These are the businesses that began by mailing paper catalogues to customers who ordered goods by mail or phone. Such businesses were required to reinvent themselves to stay competitive in the digital age by moving into the e-commerce arena, where they used the internet to reach a wide customer base and automate their ordering processes. Argos in the UK and Ireland is a prominent example of a catalogue merchant.

Virtual merchants – These companies are born digital, such as Amazon, Alibaba and eBay, and do not own any physical shops and operate only over the web. Virtual merchants may or may not hold inventory. For instance, while eBay and Alibaba do not hold inventory, Amazon allows its suppliers to use its inventory management system.

Bit vendors – These are digital merchants that deal only in digital goods, such as music, movies, games, or design templates. Key examples of such vendors are Spotify, iTunes and Netflix. The key difference between these vendors and other digital merchants is the cost of inventory. For merchants dealing in physical goods, the cost of maintaining inventory may be quite high, depending on the type of goods. For bit vendors, the variable cost of inventory (once the fixed cost is taken care of) is quite low or even close to zero, since it depends only on the number of bytes of storage required. This implies that they can carry a large range of items for delivery over the internet. However, they also have a demand side limitation in the form of the number of customers owning devices to watch videos or listen to music.

It is possible for a merchant to fit into more than one category. Amazon, for instance, is both a virtual merchant and a bit vendor (e.g., Amazon prime videos, Amazon Web Services). Such cases provide advantages in the form of a captive customer base. Amazon's strategy is to invisibly integrate relationships between merchant types enabling consumers to buy physical products via Amazon retail, view movies on Prime Videos, listen to digital music on Prime Music and download e-books seamlessly on their Kindle device. Amazon has adjusted its value proposition for sellers, rather than buyers, by offering a multitude of services and adapting the distribution process. This allows Amazon to reach customers in a wide range of ways, while simultaneously glueing the customers to their platform.

Brokering: Business Models Behind Marketplaces

However, e-commerce does not only involve selling. Digital brokers are e-commerce matchmaking platforms that bring buyers and sellers together and benefit via a fee or commission from each transaction. Based on their operations, digital brokers may be classified into seven categories.

Marketplace exchanges create business value through their actions, website functionality and platform business model. By acting as brokers who offer a service for trade in the form of intermediation between the buyers and sellers, they facilitate connections between the two. In effect, the marketplace is the product since the goods sold at the marketplace are not part of the business inventory. Orbitz is an example of such a marketplace exchange where consumers are able to search for and book flights, hotels, car rentals, cruises and vacation packages. On such brokerage sites, there are three potential factors to manage – content, reviews and other posted information and the payment system – although not every business will wish to manage them all. Some companies might prefer buyers and sellers to exchange funds directly with each other rather than put their payment system in place.

Buy/sell fulfilment – Unlike marketplace exchanges that focus on the exchange of information, buy/sell fulfilment firms also assist the parties in buying and selling. CarsDirect is one such broker that allows consumers to research, finance, purchase and insure their cars online. Respond.com is another example that connects consumers with local businesses. Amazon also provides buy/sell fulfilment service; however, it is a small part of its e-commerce ecosystem.

Demand collection systems are an interesting strategy for digital brokers. This was pioneered by travel website Priceline.com (now owned by Orbitz) with their "Name Your Price" business model. Initially trademarked and patented to prevent others in the travel industry from using the same mechanism, the model has now been adopted by other digital brokers selling travel and other goods. Under Priceline.com's "Name Your Price" model, a shopper might bid €700 for a week's holiday in France, including accommodation and travel, which, if accepted by Priceline, would be fulfilled as the broker. With margins determined by their ability to form deals with accommodation and travel vendors and in encouraging bids higher than the threshold at which they make a profit from the sale, the success of this strategy relies on an asymmetry of information, as the site does not display the actual price of the accommodation or travel to the customer.

Auction brokers conduct auctions for individuals and businesses. Their business model relies on a listing fee and a commission proportional to the value of the transaction. Auction brokers benefit from information asymmetry since the prices are kept discrete. eBay, in its initial years, completely acted as an auction broker, transitioning to marketplace exchanges in the later years (i.e., facilitating transparent pricing). Auction brokers, such as procureport.com provide reverse auction services in the B2B space when several suppliers can target a single buyer.

Transaction brokers provide third-party payment services that help in completing the monetary exchange online. Companies, including PayPal or Stripe, receive funds from the buyer and verify and transfer them to the seller after charging a small fee. The role of transaction brokers has rapidly increased in the globalised world where the buyers and sellers may be at the opposite ends of the globe. Moreover, such brokers (and digital banks, such as Revolute and TransferWise) provide e-wallets that can be used across geographies without the need for a physical card. The global mobile wallet market has been estimated at $80 billion and is expected to reach $270 billion, registering a compound annual growth rate of 15%.

Search agents collect data from multiple websites and collate it for users to compare. Google Flights, for example, acts as a search agent by curating a single page of flight prices from multiple travel websites. These agents also provide a tool that lets users change their destination on a digital map and immediately receive updated prices. While Google Flights used to charge airlines for the referrals in case of a successful booking, it halted monetising the service in early 2020. While it does not directly provide monetary benefits, Google Flights is still a rich source of data for the company. Moreover, it may also feed into another product, Google Hotels, which is still monetised.

Virtual marketplaces are the online equivalent of a shopping mall. Online marketplaces, such as Amazon, help sellers in setting up their virtual shops, listing the products, providing marketing, completing the transaction, and if need be, delivering the product. A fee is involved at each step, so the company creates value from the entire e-commerce ecosystem. This is further discussed in the following section.

4.2 Key Challenges

Making the Choice of Acting as a Marketplace

Hagiu and Wright (2013) in their article[4] entitled *Do You Really Want to Be an eBay?* Published in the Harvard Business Review illustrated the continuum between re-sellers and multi-sided platforms and the businesses in between with the advantages of both. They outline four strategic dimensions (Figure 4-C) that businesses must con-sider when deciding whether to become either a reseller or a multi-sided platform.

Figure 4-C: Four Dimensions to Consider Behind Your E-commerce Business Model. (Adapted from Hagiu & Wright, 2013)

The first dimension is the **scale effect**. If products are high-demand "blockbusters" (toilet rolls, for example), it may be better to operate as a reseller, while low-demand niche products (e.g., organic foods) may be better suited to a multi-sided platform with sellers incurring the expense of stocking and managing inventory.

---

4 Hagiu, A. & Wright, J. (2013). Do you Really Want to Be an eBay? Harvard Business Review, 91(3), 102–108.

The **aggregation effect** is the second dimension. Digital merchants aggregate products by showing additional products others have bought alongside each item viewed, such as socks with shoes. With a large selection of inventory, digital merchants can identify and offer such complementary items easily. Since they can offer products from many sellers, multi-sided platforms can take advantage of the aggregation effect. Resellers have the cost of purchasing inventory, which limits the number of complementarities they can offer.

The third dimension is the **buyer/seller experience**. This includes things such as fast delivery, a favourable returns policy and product availability. Resellers acquire more opportunities to benefit from the buyer/seller experience since they own the inventory, which provides them with greater control over the customer relationship, the quantity and quality of goods in stock and after-sales service. As multi-sided platforms facilitate interaction between buyers and sellers, they must provide tools to match up both parties. The level of interaction varies from business-to-business. On Amazon, for instance, buyers do not interact directly with sellers. Although the seller is identified on the product page, all interactions occur through Amazon's user interface. Conversely, buyers on eBay can interact with sellers through a messaging system that lets them ask questions prior to purchase.

The fourth and final dimension is **market failure**. This refers to the uncertainty surrounding product quality and the reliability of buyers or sellers on a site. For example, with AliExpress, it is most probable that the buyer does not know the seller, and so they may be wary of them and the quality or authenticity of their product. In this case, resellers have an advantage as they can monitor product quality more easily.

However, it may be noted that the classification between resellers and multi-sided platforms is not straight-jacketed and a company may lie anywhere within the continuum. For instance, one of these "hybrid" retailers is Amazon, which is a reseller for some products and a pure marketplace for others. Amazon acts as a reseller for the most demanded product, whereas it acts as a purely digital merchant for less demanded products. As Amazon fulfilment services offer sellers the added benefit of using its warehouse and shipping facilities, it can enforce quality control on the buyer/seller experience via its Prime membership program.

Apart from the four factors discussed earlier, a company's maturity and its resources are also considered crucial factors. A start-up may wish to become a reseller but might not have the working capital to purchase initial inventory, which makes being a multi-sided platform more attractive. However, as previously stated, multi-sided platforms may face chicken-and-egg, ghost town and mutual baiting problems. Recruiting potential buyers and sellers also poses a serious challenge for multi-sided platforms. This makes them dependent on sellers who are offering quality goods that keep attracting buyers and on sufficient volumes of returning buyers to maintain the site's attractiveness to sellers. Consequently, multi-sided platforms must create a trust mechanism in order to secure the quality of the relationship if the business model is to be successful, which requires huge efforts.

Hence, Hagiu and Wright (2013) note that while the multi-sided platform business model may be seductive, entrepreneurs should not overestimate its attractiveness in comparison with a more traditional reseller business model. Zappos, an e-commerce shoe retailer now owned by Amazon, is a case in point. Zappos began as a multi-sided platform but faced deep-seated customer relationship and user experience issues caused by sellers that hit consumer trust in the business. This led to the company's decision to rebuild customer confidence by becoming a reseller so that it could better monitor and manage customer relationships and user experience.

Apart from the buyer/seller relationship, the volume of sales is a significant aspect, as this determines whether developing an e-commerce site is worthwhile. If the anticipated sales volume is low, the entrepreneur may simply take advantage of Amazon's shipping infrastructure and save on the cost of establishing a dedicated platform.

Moreover, the choice between being a digital merchant and physical retailer is not mutually exclusive. A manufacturer could, for instance, establish an online shop as an additional distribution channel that is not the primary channel for selling goods. Alternatively, if a business sells mostly online, it may add physical sales alongside.

E-commerce is Efficiency-Oriented: KPIs Matter

Several of the most established digital merchants – eBay, Amazon and Alibaba – have existed for over 20 years. They were among the first to use the internet to build their customer base. They also established a well-documented set of KPIs for assessing digital merchants' performance. Such metrics enable digital merchants to understand the way in which their revenue stream is generated and structured as well as evolving in terms of volume. Generally, these are similar from one business to the next, although many companies may use additional metrics, the most common of which are listed below. Since a plethora of literature is available on e-commerce KPIs, only the most important are discussed as follows.

1. **Website KPIs** – *Unique visitors, total visits, page views, new visitors, time on site per visit, page views per visit.*

The numbers of unique visitors, total visits and page views in general indicate the attractiveness of a website's selection to customers. While new visitors may reflect the success of a new marketing campaign, returning visitors may be the results of a retargeting campaign. Time on site per visit informs the company on the level of customer engagement. Higher time on site and higher page views suggest that the visitor finds the offerings interesting and spends time on knowing more about the same.

2. **Sales KPIs** – *New customers, conversion rate, checkout abandonment, cart abandonment, checkout abandonment, total orders per day/week/month, average order value.*

The conversion rate is based on the number of new visitors versus new customers or visitors to the site who make a purchase. The number of customers depends on the conversion rate between the numbers of visits and baskets and orders created. It may be expressed as follows:

$$Conversion\ rate = (Number\ of\ Orders/Number\ of\ Visitors)*100$$

For instance, if the number of visitors on the website is 2,000 and the number of orders is 100, the conversion rate would be (100/2,000)*100 = 5%

In practice, the conversion rate varies from 0.5% to 6%, with 2% or above considered healthy.

Checkout and cart abandonment are crucial for determining the number of visitors who do not follow through with their purchases. It is estimated that digital merchants lose around $18 billion in terms of yearly sales revenue, with a cart abandonment ratio of around 70%. High cart abandonment reflects possible issues with the shipping cost, delivery time, payment method or technical issues that must be sorted by companies.

Amazon's login system is one way of payment and shipping processes, enabling faster checkout by using saved customer details to remove the need to re-enter address and payment details. This can also help in avoiding cart abandonment – online shoppers frequently add items to their carts, see the total price and shipping time, and abandon the transaction, leaving the site without any purchase. By showing total shipped costs and delivery times on product information pages, Amazon helps prevent the notion of cart abandonment.

The total number of orders per day, week or month is important for business, along with the average order value. With average order value, companies can gain insight into their pricing and selling approaches. For instance, if a company sells a product at four different price points ($15, $25, $35 and $50), and the average order value is around $20, it may be said that most orders are in the lower range and of a single unit of product. In this case, the company may opt for cross-selling or up-selling strategies.

3. **Operational KPIs** – *return rate, gross margin, order turnaround time, open cases.*

High return rates or numerous open customer service cases suggest problems with the products themselves or after-sales management. While the return rate for brick-and-mortar stores is estimated at around 10%, for e-commerce, the return is estimated to be double at 20%. This is a dual cost for the company, first being the forgone revenue due to the cancellation of sales, while second being logistic costs in acquiring the product back. Hence, the companies keep an eye on the return rate to ensure that they do not lose substantial amounts of money due to excessive returns.

Interestingly, many companies have used lenient return policies as a marketing tool. Zappos and Amazon have a lenient and simple return policy with virtually no onus on the customer to "prove" any problem with the product or the delivery. This results in a higher level of trust in the company, and the customer does not think twice before ordering with the company.

4. **Digital Marketing KPIs** – *Facebook* "talking about this" *and new likes, Twitter retweets and new followers, Amazon ratings, open rate, click rate, conversion rate, referral sources (percent from search, direct, e-mail, pay-per-click), pay-per-click cost per acquisition, pay-per-click total conversations.*

Since the beginning of digital marketing, online display advertising and search engine optimisation remain the top two choices for marketers. Measuring the pay-per-click cost, the cost-per-acquisition or the total conversion rate remain significant as they indicate the success of digital marketing campaigns. However, recently, social media have emerged as the next preferred channel for marketers since 2017. Consequently, social media marketing metrics, such as likes, mentions and follows have become useful KPIs for digital merchants. Nonetheless, businesses also employ techniques such as sentiment analysis to ensure positive word-of-mouth (WoM) as well as keeping eye on whether their brand is trending for wrong reasons. Apart from social media, WoM is also measured by traditional KPIs, including ratings, reviews and referral sources.

4.3 Key Takeaways and Further Considerations

1. A variety of business models for digital merchants, from pure resellers to multi-sided platforms, exist. A company may choose to confine itself within a specific business model (e.g., Zappos) or use a hybrid business model (e.g., Amazon).
2. Digital merchants often draw from the long tail of retail, i.e., selling a wide variety of low-popularity items to a lot of different people by covering all the niche markets.
3. KPI measurements play a key role in performance measurement and operations of digital merchants.

Do You Have an Integrated Touchpoint Architecture?

In the long run, digital merchants must overcome two problems if they wish to remain successful. The first is how to differentiate themselves from other digital merchants. A digital merchant will not have the traction required to successfully launch without a unique selling point associated with a product, user experience or customer loyalty, thereby making it stand out from competitors. This is a continuous exercise since the uniqueness does not last forever. Etsy, for example, once stood out as a marketplace for handcrafted goods. It now has several competitors, including Amazon.

The second problem is commoditisation. How can businesses differentiate themselves if the product or service they offer is standardised? Platforms selling flight tickets encounter this issue. As the product remains the same everywhere, ease of the buying process (SEO & UX) and price are the only differentiators. Since price primarily influences buyers' decision-making, quality of user experience, post-sale support, shipping time and other factors have a minute effect on revenue generation. In this situation, the only way to maximise revenue is through volume of sales rather than holding a large inventory selection.

Provided the convergence of e-commerce and ever-expanding ecosystems of products and services, many businesses seek to answer the question of the possibility for a digital merchant to differentiate itself. Trust impacts consumer experience and the relationship between the business and the customers. Hence, entrepreneurs must decide whether to offer personal shopping services and post-sale contact or consumer support. While customer journey is not a new tool in marketing, it gains a new meaning in digital context as digital merchants need to design different touch points during a customer journey.

Originally proposed by Procter & Gamble in the early 2000s, "moment-of-truth" refers to key customer interaction with the product and service. Earlier versions of the customer journey focused on the moment of purchase (the first moment-of-truth) and the consumption (the second moment-of-truth) of the product or service. In a digital context, the first moment of truth leads to merchants being experts in digital design to maximise conversion. Amazon's "1-Click" button for ordering minimises customers' effort. The 1-Click button was key in providing Amazon with a competitive advantage. R. Polk Wagner, a professor at the University of Pennsylvania Law School and an expert on patent law, explains: "It allowed Amazon to show customers that there was a good reason to give them their data and the permission to charge them on an incremental basis. It opened other avenues for Amazon in e-commerce. That is the real legacy of the 1-Click patent."[5] Hence, the 1-Click button was exceptionally patented, as the entire process as opposed to a specific single invention gave Amazon two major competitive advantages. It provided Amazon with a database of customer payment and preference information that no other retailer or Internet website could compete with. Second, the 1-Click process helped to minimise shopping cart abandonment by making the purchase fast and frictionless, leading to a dramatic increase in the conversion rate.

---

5 https://knowledge.wharton.upenn.edu/article/amazons-1-click-goes-off-patent/ as accessed May 20, 2022.

The advent of digital technology added at least two other steps: one moment before and one moment after. The moment before the purchase, termed zero moment-of-truth by Google, refers to when customers search online regarding the product or service. This means that merchants must adeptly use Search Engine Optimisation (SEO) and Search Engine Advertisement (SEA) to become amongst the first on the Search Engine Results Page (SERP) on the path-to-purchase of the Internet user. There are about ten organics (non-paid) results on every SERP and between three and six advertised (paid) results. Several studies have analyzed how consumers engage with the SERPs based on different keywords. Those studies reveal that the first organic search result yields amazing results (Click-Through-Rate of 19% to 30% on average). Being on the first SERP, either via organic results or paid results, is the condition sine-qua-non for driving traffic to the website.

The moment following the consumption, termed third moment-of-truth, refers to when customers share their experience on social media. It's linked to the power of Peer-to-Peer (P2P), which is deemed to be one the most efficient ways of advertising products. According to a recent report from Kantar Media,[6] 93% of consumers trust friends and family as a source of information regarding brands. This is to be contrasted with advertising, which is the least trusted at only 28%. Retailers can leverage this using referral programs wherein they credit existing customers points, cash, or discount for each invited friend who makes a purchase. A good example of P2P marketing. It is these moments of truth that digital merchants must also manage successfully.

Moreover, as Muzellec and O'Raghallaigh (2018) argue, recent advances in mobile technology have resulted in ubiquitous moment-of-truths that occur simultaneously, often on the same device. In other words, all four stages – search, purchase, consumption, and sharing – may happen within a single set of transactions. Moreover, modern retail is increasingly becoming channel agnostic, with a need for a consistent experience across online, mobile and offline channels. This calls for an integrated touchpoint architecture across customer journeys that also integrate Delivery and Return (see Figure 4-D).

Amazon app is an excellent example of such ubiquitous moment-of-truth and integrated touchpoint architecture. Instead of searching on a search engine, customers directly visit the app or the website to search for the product or service. They are then able to compare across offerings and make purchase decisions. Oftentimes, their contact and payment details are saved on the platform, making purchasing just a matter of clicks. While physical products would take time to get delivered, digital products (such as eBook or a Game) would be available instantly. At the end of the transaction, the customer can rate the product as well as the vendor. Moreover, if they are not happy with their purchase, the same app or website can be used to cancel the

---

6 See Kantar Report on Media & Me, as accessed on May 2022.

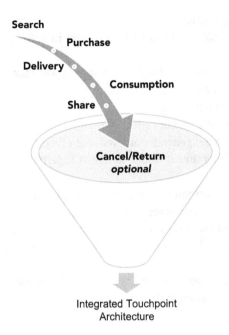

Integrated Touchpoint
Architecture

Figure 4-D: Towards an Integrated Touchpoint Architecture.

order or return the product. Thus, by providing an integrated touchpoint architecture, the company keeps the customer on its platform.

Google runs a think tank that offers insight into the way the internet affects buyers' decision process. This demonstrates that e-commerce sites must understand their buyers' decision-making process, such as whether a mobile is important to them and their location when they are looking for the information. They must also note if they are buying for "now", such as when booking an Uber cab while standing on a sidewalk, or buying for "future", such as when arranging holiday accommodation in two months' time.

Understanding a buyer's location and motivations helps e-commerce businesses reach them at the right moment in their decision process. If they are to prioritise the devices and services appropriately, businesses must know when these "I want to go", "I want to do", or "I want to buy" moments are.

Until recently, purchasing clothing online seemed illogical to shoppers due to worries over fit and quality. It was the same with fresh produce. How could food stay cool if delivered when the customer was not at home? However, thanks to e-commerce innovations, buying clothing and fresh food online is now commonplace.

Naturale was one of the first e-commerce companies to sell online fresh produce in France and the UK when it launched in 2000. To deliver fish as fresh as customers could get at the seaside, the company was required to overcome the supply chain challenge of first transporting fresh food and then keeping it in perfect condition between delivery and the customer arriving home. In order to accomplish that, Naturale developed a container that kept food cold for up to 48 hours, even in extreme heat.

As you might expect, the average cost of ordering food from Naturale was much higher than buying from a local supermarket for several reasons.

- Fresh products generally cost more than packaged items.
- Naturale was selling premium products at a higher price.
- To reduce shipping cost-per-item, customers generally ordered more food at one time so the cost of weekly shops was higher than it would be from a supermarket.

Despite this, Naturale was able to build its customer base as its climate-controlled containers kept product quality high, and the customers came to trust the brand. They also appreciated the convenience, time savings and the appeal of not having to grocery shop in the evenings or at weekends. Such positive experiences lock-in customers and generate recurring business.

For Naturale, understanding the "I want to buy" and the "I want to do" moments of their customers were key to the successful launch of their business.

5 "Social" at the Core of a Digital Business: Valuing Audience or the Community?

This chapter discusses the value creation and value capture strategies of social platforms. Our appellation of social platforms allows us to include services, such as Facebook, Twitter, LinkedIn, Instagram, Snapchat, YouTube, TikTok, and WhatsApp, which are sometimes referred to as social media, social network, and communication apps. These are defined and described in the first section. We then explain that social platform business models share the common characteristics of monetising a group of users, i.e., a community or an audience and/or its data. We finally expand on the ethical tensions arising from locking in a key resource such as an audience to derive financial return from the "actual" customers, viz., the advertisers.

5.1 Social: From Latin *socius*, "Friend"

Social media and social networks are often used indifferently. In this section, we differentiate and define social media, social networks, and communication apps. We then explain their common value architecture design, which rests on their ability to capture and monetise data from their users.

Here, Social is the common adjective. Social comes from the Latin *socialis,* "allied", or from *socius,* "friend". Media and network do not mean the same.

Hence, social media are primarily media – i.e., means of communication of content (e.g., information and entertainment) to people. The social element describes the notion that contrary to traditional media, social media users can generate content and/or react to the content that they consume by liking, sharing, and commenting. YouTube is a good example of social media (that is not a social network). Similarly, social networks are primarily networks, i.e., a group or system of interconnected people who communicate with one another and may form an online community; social networks describe a digital platform that allows peer-to-peer communication through an open system.

Facebook, LinkedIn, Instagram, and TikTok had different starting points; yet, nowadays, they may all be considered both social networks and social media. The media dimension–content delivered to the right audience through a powerful algorithm – is gradually becoming more essential than the network attribute.

More recent platforms like TikTok or Snapchat can be considered social media distributing vertically oriented content since it is mobile-first. TikTok was created from the ashes of what was once Musical.ly, a social media app used to share short lip–sync videos. TikTok reached over 1 billion active users per month in September 2021. The network structure resembles a vertical content distribution system, comprised of influencers at the top of the pyramid.

Facebook started as a network, but the media dimension of the platform has gradually become increasingly prominent. Users may have originally joined Facebook to communicate with their friends and peers. This is less the case today. Facebook users log on to the platform to consume entertaining or informative content produced mainly by institutional contributors and distributed to them through an algorithmic "Newsfeed".

To communicate with peers, users of Facebook have turned to WhatsApp and Messenger. Hence, the network attribute is now primarily assumed by what we will call peer-to-peer communication apps such as WhatsApp, Weebo, and Messenger. Those apps operate as one-to-one communication services or as a closed network (group), vis-a-vis Facebook or Twitter that are more open in their setting. Similarly, some of these peer-to-peer communication platforms have a very heavy media component such as Snap Chat.

To summarise, social media are primarily providers of content which is curated (share), endorsed (like), or remarked upon (comments) by an audience, while Social Networks and Communication Apps primarily rest on a community of people who communicate and share content in an open (Social Network) or closed (communication app) manner. Conceptually, social networks, social media, and peer-to-peer communication apps are therefore different, but in practice, platforms such as Facebook, TikTok, Snap Chat, Instagram, and Pinterest have evolved over time and embrace features and characteristics of the three constructs. From a business model perspective, most of the social platforms share the same value architecture; they provide value to different sides – mainly users or a B2C side and advertisers or a B2B side.

The B2C side is a group of users who share and consume content in the form of text, images, or video. These users provide data (demographic and psychographic information) or generate data through their interactions (metadata). Some social platforms directly capture value from their users in the form of social commerce and premium versions. Yet, the data generated by the audience can be useful for advertising purposes but may sometimes be sold to third parties. Hence, the most prominent value capture mechanism involves a B2B side.

5.2 Audience: Monetising Attention and Data

The most common revenue model for social platforms is advertising. The platform creates value through its ability to present ad content to the right targeted audience. This optimised advertising technique rests on the exploitation of data from the audience. Hence, the business model of social media rests initially on audience acquisition.

Production of an Audience

In the Social Networks movie (2010), Sean Parker (founder of Napster) is reportedly discussing with Mark Zuckerberg and his then associate Eduardo Saverin. The latter is concerned about the Facebook business model (or lack of it) and wants to run ads. The former reassures Facebook founders: "Right now, Facebook is cool, and you don't want to ruin it with ads because ads aren't cool". Growing the audience is what matters at this early stage. No audience, no product; no product, no revenue. It must be considered in sequence. The oft-repeated adage – "if it is free, then you are the product" – is the perfect description of this business model in which end-users can benefit from a "free" service (connecting with peers) but it is at the price of being transformed as an audience to be sold to a business side. With an audience, there are no reciprocal connections. When audiences generate data, they create value that can be monetised for advertisers. So, though Facebook provides its audience with tools they can use to connect as a community, it has also been monetising its audience right from the start. The following graph (Figure 5-A) shows the lag between audience and revenue. The audience initially grew much faster than revenue, culminating in a 300% growth in the number of active users in 2010, and from 2013 onwards, revenue grew much faster than users.

Social networks are considered multi-sided platforms (see Chapter 2). As such, they need a strong value proposition on the users' side. For Facebook, the initial value proposition emphasised the network aspects of social media: "Connect with friends and the world around you" along with the tagline "It's free and always will be" (which changed to "It's quick and easy" in August 2019). The tagline emphasises the ease of adoption and user experience. The slogan "connect with friends . . ." illuminates the success of Facebook, which can partially be attributed to a same-side Network effect.

Valuing Network Effects

The Network effect means that the usefulness of the social network increases as the number of users increases. With almost 3 billion users, the network effect has given Facebook a huge competitive advantage. For a while, Facebook protected its dominant position whenever a social network with a similar value proposition tried to challenge it. This can be illustrated through the failed attempt of Google + to defy Facebook in 2010. G + project's slogan was "Real-life sharing rethought for the web", as the design team sought to replicate the way people interact offline more closely than on other social networking services, such as Facebook and Twitter. Many commentators conceded that G + digital design and UX were indeed more intuitive than Facebook. However, due to the same-side network effect, the service never really took off. The few users who were initially enticed by the digital design

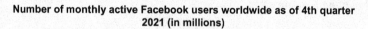

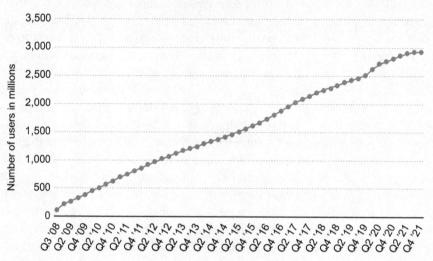

Sources
Facebook; Meta Platforms
© Statista 2022

Additional Information:
Worldwide; Meta Platforms; Q3 2008 to Q4 2021

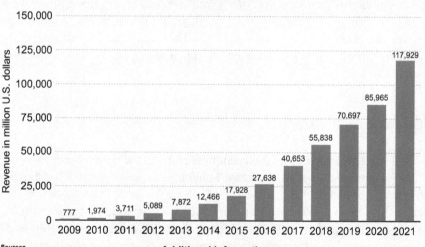

Sources
Facebook; Meta Platforms
© Statista 2022

Additional Information:
Worldwide; Meta Platforms; 2009 to 2021

Figure 5-A: User Acquisition and Monetisation for Facebook.
(Source: Statista 2022)

and UX of Google + became rapidly disillusioned with the service, as none of their friends was active on the network. On April 2, 2019, Google + definitely shut down. This effect and its reinforcing mechanisms such as brand habit and high switching costs are described in Figure 5-B. The same effect has so far protected WhatsApp from competitors such as Signals. Telegram, with 550 million monthly active users (an increase of 175% since 2018), may now be reaching a critical number of users to sustain its own network effect.

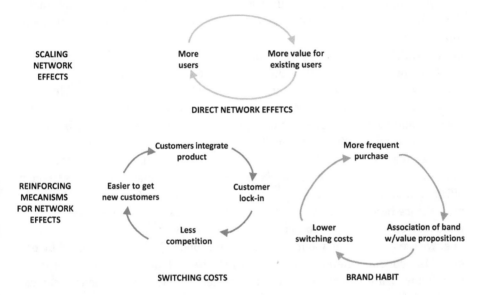

Figure 5-B: Network Effects Explained.

Keeping the Users Engaged Through Content

As explained earlier, users of social networks and media engage with content and/ or with peers. The role of the digital algorithm is then to serve the right content including paid content–i.e., advertisements, to the right audience. Thus, the main challenge for an audience-based business model is to develop the toolbox that entices the users to spend more time on the platform.

To do so, advertising is meshed with other forms of content. Content can be generated by peers, influencers, or brands. The motivation to produce content for peers is social/ peer endorsement of their way of living, while both influencers and brands have a direct or indirect financial incentive. For them, this is largely a communication activity, which is now called content marketing: the process of planning, creating, distributing, sharing, and publishing content in videos, pictures, or text format on social media, blogs, websites, etc. Influencers and brands produce diverse types of informative or entertaining content. Native advertising, also called sponsored content, is a type of advertising that matches the form and function of the platform upon which it appears. In many cases, it functions like an advertorial and manifests as a video, article, or editorial.

Regardless of the format, the goal is to meet a marketing strategy objective: reach a target audience and increase brand awareness, sales, engagement, and loyalty. The main function of the social platform is to match engaging (and sometimes paid) content to individual users through an algorithm. The algorithm is a compilation of rules and data that cast extrapolations about what users want to (and therefore will) see on the platform. Social media sites create unique algorithms for every person, which means no two people will have exactly the same social media feed.

This ultra-individualisation makes social media content highly addictive. The Fear of Missing Out can further generate addictive behaviour. The table below shows the relationship between the average time spent on social media, the yearly revenue, and the number of active users of the principal social platforms in 2021.

The table reveals that social media platforms grab a lot of our attention. If communication apps such as WhatsApp have some difficulty in monetising this attention, social platforms such as Facebook, Instagram, or Snapchat seem extremely efficient in keeping users engaged and exposing them to lucrative ads. Hence, for an audience-based business model, a key challenge is to entice the users to spend more time on the platform so that the platform derives additional advertising revenue. We are now talking about the "Attention Economy". The term, coined by psychologist-economist Herbert A. Simon in 1971, treats human attention as a scarce commodity. With the emergence of the Internet, it is now treated as the management of information and considered the New Currency of Business (Davenport & Beck 2001).[1]

To capture users' attention, platforms are experts in UX and digital design (Remember Facebook's motto: "It's quick and easy"). Scrolling or swiping makes users move vertically or horizontally, respectively, towards a bottomless feed. There is always increasingly more content (funny videos, interesting news . . .) to be discovered further down the feed. Not surprisingly, scrolling has been criticised for its addictiveness. Attention constitutes the token users' flap in the hope of uncovering rewards. To scroll is to take a chance, just like with roulette or a slot machine. It is this aspect of scrolling behaviour that is now associated with problematic addictive behaviour like gambling.

---

1 Davenport, T. H. & Beck, J. C. (2001). The Attention Economy. Ubiquity, 2001(May), 1-es.

Table 5-A: Attention, Active Users, and Revenue.

Name of the platform	Number of monthly active users (in billion)	Average daily time per user in hours	Yearly revenue (in billions)	Average rev per user and per hour
Facebook	2.92	1	117	3.34
YouTube	2.3	2.4	28.8	0.43
WhatsApp	2	0.6	0.7	0.05
Instagram	1	0.48	17.4	3.02
TikTok	1.2	0.83	1.9	0.10
Snapchat	0.53	0.1	4.86	7.64

[Source: Estimated figures compiled from Statista, Backkinko.com, BusinessofApps, Techjury.net, CNBC & SimilarWeb (2021)]

5.3 A Business System for Advertisers and Influencers

Social platforms have developed a huge competitive advantage over traditional media, which rests on the smart use of the data generated by the audience. More recent networks (e.g., Instagram and TikTok) also rely heavily on influencers, who are both heavy users and business partners of the platforms.

Advertisers: Leveraging Data for a Targeted Audience

As seen earlier, the presence of a large audience on social media constitutes the essential element of the business model, as individual users are consumers (and to a lesser extent the producers) of free content, and they also provide the raw material or key resource (data) for value creation. When audiences generate data, they create a key resource that can be used to offer value-added services to advertisers. Data are essential to feed the right content to users and facilitate granular targeting for advertisers. The role of digital algorithms is then to serve the right advertisements to the right audience, based on the criteria established by the advertisers.

To narrow down the targeting options, the toolbox for marketers is packed with data. Facebook, for example, generates four petabytes of data per day – that's a million gigabytes!!! Most of it is simply stored by Facebook for the perusal of its users but a sizable proportion will be used for marketing purposes. We can distinguish at least two types of data.

First, there is the demographic data pertaining to the users, such as who they are (age, gender, and personal status), where they are from (country, city), and what they like (interest-based likes and brand-following activity). Some of this data is self-declared (gender, marital status), and some is generated by the users without necessarily being aware of it: geo-localisation, browsing behaviour, device usage, etc. Every time we friend someone on Instagram, watch a video YouTube recommends for us, post a status, or share someone's tweet, metadata – data about the data – is at work in the background. This data is seldom sold to a third party as it would not be very well perceived by users and is not very astute from a business perspective. Instead, the platform keeps the data to develop sophisticated toolboxes for their business clients. For example, Facebook Audience Insights is a tool developed by Meta to provide advertisers aggregated information about people on Facebook and more particularly people who like their page, so that they can easily find more people like their existing audience.

Then, there is the data generated by the campaign itself. Here, social media platforms provide advertisers with data about their campaign such as Click through rate and Reach, average video watch time, etc. These metrics enable advertisers to monitor reach and impressions, evaluate engagement rate, CPC and CPM, track referrals, measure bounce rates or conversion rates, and eventually Return on Ad Spend (ROAS). In essence, the data allows advertisers to perform two key tasks: reach a well-targeted audience with a tailored message and accurately measure the return on advertising (ROA). These two characteristics make social media advertising a form of promotion that surpasses the performance of any other media. Social media advertising combines the virtue of mass marketing–unlimited reach, often more than one billion!– and the advantages of one-to-one marketing (micro-targeting and tailored messages).

Influencers: A Hybrid User-Customer for Social Platforms

As seen earlier, the same-side network effect can be very strong on social networks (e.g., Facebook initial configuration), while the cross-side network effect seems to be more prevalent with social media (e.g., YouTube). The evolution and relative decline in Facebook use can be attributed to the users primarily joining the platform to engage with peers. Advertisers who operate on the other side were there only to subsidise the free use of the platform. Too often and despite their effort to produce engaging content, advertisers were perceived as disrupting the flow and experience of users.

More recently, marketing on social platforms has been mediated by super users or influencers. According to influencermarketinghub.com, Instagram is the network of choice for influencer marketing campaigns, with 79% of the brands considering it their most important platform. Reflecting the evolution of its business ecosystem, Facebook's preference for influencer marketing has increased from 7% to 50% between 2018 and 2021, according to The State of Influencer Marketing 2021 research. TikTok and YouTube are the two other destinations for influencer marketing.

Influencers are in fact the supercharged buyer persona of a particular target audience. Hence, psychologically, they can be perceived as being on the same side as users. Yet, they too use the tools initially designed for businesses and are clients of the social platforms.

Instagram and TikTok now propose two types of professional accounts: a Creator account which is "best for public figures, content producers, artists and influencers" or a business account "best for retailers, local businesses, brands, organisations and service providers". Users with Business or Creator Accounts have access to Analytics. Analytics provide insight into top-performing videos and follower engagement. With a Creator Account, you can see Post Insights, run ads, sort your inbox, and create shoppable posts.

5.4 Ethical Concerns over the Attention/Data-Driven Business Model

Social platforms have been criticised by activists, community leaders, and political representatives for several reasons. In this section, we highlight three of the most prominent tensions that epitomise the ethical concerns inherent in social platform business models. These include the use of personal data, the addictive nature of social media, and the role of algorithms in shaping our worldview.

Users' Privacy vs. Data-Driven Business Model

Advertising is an extremely powerful strategy for monetising an audience. Yet, it has some negative effects. In the example of a social network (i.e., Facebook original setting), users join the network to form a community. The community is defined by a reciprocal exchange of all happenings on the same side. Ads, which are the emanation of business from the other side of the platforms, are simply there to subsidise the model. They do not provide added value to the users; on the contrary, they rely on data to better target the users. Hence, the inconvenience of the ad as well as users' personal data are the price users "pay" for using the service for free.

This leads to tensions over data usage. Data has now surpassed oil as "the world's most valuable resource". Yet, end-users consider personal data as intimate and private. Hence, it is not surprising that privacy, defined as the ability of the individual to control the terms under which personal information is acquired and used (Westin, 1968),[2] is a source of tension. Online privacy behaviour falls into three main categories, according to Bartsch and Dienlin (2016):[3]

---

2 Westin, A. F. (1968). Privacy and Freedom. Washington and Lee Law Review, 25(1), 166.
3 Bartsch, M. & Dienlin, T. (2016). Control your Facebook: An Analysis of Online Privacy Literacy. Computers in Human Behavior, 56, 147–154.

- **Informational** – how much information we share.
- **Social** – how many people we allow access to that information, and
- **Psychological** – the intimacy of that shared information.

The intimate relations that users have with their personal data, combined with the pivotal role of users' data in social network revenue models, inherently leads to some tensions that may result in crisis.

Facebook has come under scrutiny due to a series of high-profile data breaches and related privacy crises. These have shaken user confidence in social platforms' ability to protect users' information and highlighted users' lack of knowledge about how their data is used. Users seem ill-informed about the specific type of data collected, the purpose thereof and the identity of the collector. Despite this, they remain reluctant to change their online privacy behaviour, limit their online activity, or the unthinkable, quit their "internet lives" (Bradley, 2005).[4] This apparent detachment between online privacy concerns and actual online privacy behaviour, known as the privacy paradox, has been explored extensively (Gerber et al., 2018;[5] Barth & deJong, 2017;[6] Kokolakis, 2017[7]).

However, in some cases, users do react, as illustrated by the rise of ad blocking technology adoption, rising from approximately 21 M users in 2010 to more than 180 M users worldwide in 2019. According to e-Marketers, in the US alone, over 75 M users had ad blocker software installed on their browsers in 2020.

The recent and relative success of apps such as Signal and Telegram – both considered less greedy with data and more respectful of privacy than Meta-Owned WhatsApp, is also symptomatic of users' scepticism towards ad/data-based business models.

Users' Mental Health vs. Attention Economy

As mentioned earlier, users' attention is what all digital and non-digital advertisers are competing for. The advertisers' job (on TV, outdoor, and digital) is to grab people's attention – and attention is a scarce resource. Of the twenty-four hours in

---

4 Bradley, K. (2005). Internet Lives: Social Context and Moral Domain in Adolescent Development. New Directions for Youth Development, 2005(108), 57–76.
5 Gerber, N., Gerber, P., & Volkamer, M. (2018). Explaining the Privacy Paradox: A Systematic Review of Literature Investigating Privacy Attitude and Behavior. Computers & Security, 77, 226–261.
6 Barth, S. & De Jong, M. D. (2017). The Privacy Paradox–Investigating Discrepancies between Expressed Privacy Concerns and Actual Online Behavior–A Systematic Literature Review. Telematics and Informatics, 34(7), 1038–1058.
7 Kokolakis, S. (2017). Privacy Attitudes and Privacy Behaviour: A Review of Current Research on the Privacy Paradox Phenomenon. Computers & Security, 64, 122–134.

a day, while a third is dedicated to sleep, the rest is packed with all the other activities (work, commute, sports, eating, childcare, etc.): competition for attention is thus fierce. The business model of digital advertising implies that once hooked, the user must be kept on screen, if possible. To do so, social platforms have become UX experts. The websites and apps of YouTube, Instagram, and Facebook are so well designed that they may generate addictive behaviour.

According to Addiction Center,[8] as many as 5 to 10% of Americans meet the criteria for social media addiction today. Social media addiction can be largely attributed to the dopamine-inducing social environments that social networking sites provide. Studies have shown that the constant stream of retweets, likes, shares and other forms of self-disclosing behaviour on social media ignites the brain's reward area which is also triggered when consuming an addictive substance like Cocaine. Of course, addiction is an extreme situation, and very often, social media is only the catalyst for deeper personal issues. Amongst the most widely recognised causes of addiction to social media are low self-esteem and hyperactivity, or even lack of affection, a deficiency that young adults and teenagers try to replace with famous social media likes.

Besides addiction, there may be some negative relationship between social media and well-being. In a recent review titled "Social media use and well-being: What we know and what we need to know", Patti M. Valkenburg (2022) showed[9] that general social media usage was associated with higher levels of depression/depressive symptoms and anxiety (e.g., Yoon, Kleinman, Mertz & Brannick, 2019[10]), but, again surprisingly, also with higher happiness levels (e.g., Liu, Baumeister, Yang, & Hu, 2019[11]).

Filter Bubble (Mirror) vs. Democracy (Window)

Finally, the algorithms used to match the content to users are also a source of concern. As stated, the main aim of the platform is to provide the users with what he/she wants to read or watch (personalised content) so that he/she remains engaged, if possible. This has led to a situation, called the filter bubble, in which the users are exposed only to information and opinions that conform to and reinforce their

---

8 https://www.addictioncenter.com/drugs/social-media-addiction/ as accessed on April 11, 2022.
9 Valkenburg, P. M. (2022). Social Media Use and Well-Being: What We Know and What We Need to Know. Current Opinion in Psychology, 45.
10 Yoon, S .M. (2019). Is Social Network Site Usage Related to Depression? A Meta-Analysis of Facebook–Depression Relations Journal of Affective Disorder, 248, 65–72.
11 Liu, D., Baumeister, R. F., Yang, C.-c., & Hu, B. (2019). Digital Communication Media Use and Psychological Well-Being: A Meta-Analysis. Journal of Computer-Mediated Communication, 24, 259–274.

own beliefs. The personalised function of the algorithm can be praised when dealing with individual tastes and hobbies (give the people who enjoy watching cats, the opportunity to watch more cats). It is also generally well accepted when the content is commercial or branded: most consumers would rather be subjected to the advertisement of products and services they enjoy, rather than irrelevant ads. Personalisation is a bias that can be positive and pleasant.

The issue is that social platforms, in particular Facebook, Twitter, and YouTube, have gradually replaced newspapers and television channels as our main source of information. The information we see from these media is biased, based on our personal preferences. These preferences are inferred from our browsing history, age, gender, location, and other data. The result is a flood of articles and posts that support our current opinions and perspectives, to ensure that we enjoy what we see. The internet was initially presented as an open window to the rest of the world: Facebook's original slogan was "Making the world more open and connected". However, thanks to this biased algorithm, our mobile screen functions more as a deforming mirror of our own perception of the world. This affects not only political views and analysis: universalist views vs. nationalist views, pro-choice vs. pro-life, etc. It also affects the types of information we may be exposed to. Hence, someone initially concerned about immigration might see more and more articles and news related to this topic while someone initially concerned about gay rights or racial discrimination will also be exposed to more news pertaining to these topics. Hence, for one audience, immigration can be seen as a major issue while for another, race relations are more prominent. This leads to a widening democratic gap, where not only are we incapable of listening to the other side's argument, but may not even agree anymore on the topics that need to be discussed.

5.5 The Rise of Social Commerce

To overcome the limitations of audience-based business, social platforms are turning to other methods for generating revenue. The most prominent new revenue stream is e-commerce.

Social platforms can be seen as intermediaries between some professional users (brands, influencers) and many individuals. They mainly facilitate the exchange of information. Gradually, however, platforms are becoming marketplaces that also facilitate transactions in goods and services in exchange for money.

The add-on e-commerce feature provides a streamlined in-app product selling experience to both businesses and individual users. By doing so, it further locks in users and businesses, while providing the platforms with an additional source of revenue.

The global social commerce market size was valued at $584.91 billion in 2021 and is projected to grow at a whopping 30.8% compound annual growth rate from 2022 to 2030! Despite the robust growth, the United States and Europe lag China, which has been a leader in social commerce, with some 424 million people making purchases on platforms such as WeChat in 2021.

Facebook, Pinterest, Instagram, and TikTok all provide shopping abilities, all with some slight variations. Pinterest shopping is fully integrated with the user experience. Users enter the product they are looking for in the search bar at the top of the home feed and then they click on the Shop tab at the top of the search results to browse and buy the product.

Unlike other listing sites like eBay, Facebook Marketplace allows businesses (and consumers) to list items for free. To compensate for this potential loss of revenue, Facebook turns again to advertisement through boosted listings. This time, however, the ad is unlikely to annoy users, as they are searching precisely for the item being boosted. In this regard, it functions a bit like Google AdWords, which places on the top of the search engine results page an ad matching the search query. There is a clear synergy between the need of the users/buyers and the offering (boosted listings).

Facebook's newest e-commerce feature, Shops, launched in 2020, allows small businesses to feature product catalogues on their Facebook and Instagram profiles, and for followers to purchase in-app. Brands are seeing huge results, including some seeing 66% higher-order values through shops than from their websites.

Indeed, social commerce presents itself as a real alternative revenue model for social networks and is very well placed to gain significant market share over traditional e-commerce websites. It engages users in a more meaningful way, as it is more experiential. Instagram, TikTok, and Pinterest are experience-driven channels that enable shopping within a live streaming experience. Unique content created by brands, influencers, or individuals drives authentic discovery, engagement, and action. Action (purchase) is the last and the natural step of the users' journey. The old advertising model was called AIDA (Attention, Interest, Desire, and Action) but implied diverse types of advertisement at different phases of the customer journey. What's more, the action (purchase) was never fully measured and could not be related to the advertisement that had initially driven the attention or the desire: "Half the money I spend on advertising is wasted; the trouble is I don't know which half". This is no longer the case with social commerce, which allows consumers to close the loop on their journey by providing an end-to-end experience for users.

In sum, social commerce presents a significant future stream of revenue for social networks, as it overcomes some of the limitations of traditional ads by providing an immediate and clear return on investment. It also has the potential to seriously challenge traditional e-commerce transactional models, as it provides a more immersive, end-to-end experience for the buyer.

5.6 Key Takeaways and Further Considerations

1. The business model of social networks is based on developing a sense of community; however, the social media business model is based on monetising an audience (data of many individuals).
2. Social networks and media focus on the content and may rely on partners such as influencers to persuade the community to spend more time on the platform and to keep them engaged.
3. Social platforms' business models inherently create tensions and ethical dilemmas between a community of free users and the necessity to derive revenue from that community.

Will the Community Pay?

As seen in this chapter, the audience-based business models present some challenges. Increasingly, other sources of revenue are being considered. We have already talked about social commerce, which has gained significant momentum. A Subscription revenue model is also an option, while the business model of communication Apps such as Messenger and WhatsApp still needs refinement.

To overcome the challenges of audience-based business models, social platforms could stop using advertising and turn to freemium. LinkedIn has been offering a premium version of its membership to users right from its inception. YouTube has had subscription and ad-free options since 2014. More recently, in January 2022, both Instagram and TikTok announced that they have begun testing subscriptions with a limited number of US creators through subscriber lives, stories, and badges.

LinkedIn was launched in 2003, and from the beginning, had a relatively clear value proposition. It was thought of as a social network platform where professionals can find and list jobs—in other words, a Facebook for professionals. Three key segments had traditionally constituted the users of LinkedIn. Businesses could develop a LinkedIn company page to present themselves. They could also advertise their products and services via LinkedIn Marketing Solutions. Recruiters and HR specialists constituted a sub-segment. They had specific recruitment needs, addressed by LinkedIn Recruitment solutions. Similar to multi-sided platforms, those two business segments were paying customers. Individual users are LinkedIn members who use the network to connect with other professionals and display their professional abilities through a personal page like an online CV. This last category of users constitutes the free users. As for Facebook and other social networks, members are the foundation and the key resource that allow LinkedIn to monetise its offering to businesses. However, in November 2005, LinkedIn Corporation launched two new subscription offerings: Pro and Personal Plus. If the Pro accounts provided a simple upgrade path for recruiters and other existing Business account holders,

Personal Plus accounts were aimed at individuals and job seekers. In its initial business plan, the company had no intention of charging individual users. Yet, after a few months of existence, LinkedIn realised that a small proportion of individual users was willing to pay for additional features such as allowing potential clients or employers to contact them without having to purchase InMails or ask their connections for introductions. Since its acquisition by Microsoft in 2016, LinkedIn has been gradually evolving into a Customer Relationship Management Service, which in many aspects, competes with Salesforce. Today, LinkedIn has over 774 million registered members from over 200 countries worldwide.

More recently, subscription models for individual users take two forms.

In the first scenario, it is the platform itself that offers the subscription in exchange for a reduction of pain and/or additional features. It is the model followed by YouTube, which allows any of its users to use its website without the inconvenience of advertisements. YouTube Premium subscription, which was initially launched in 2014 but exists in its current format since 2018, allows users to watch videos on YouTube without advertisements across all of its website and mobile apps, including YouTube Music, YouTube Gaming, and YouTube Kids apps. YouTube subscription works as a pain reliever: "Watch videos uninterrupted by ads, while using other apps or when the screen is locked" as well as offering additional features "Save videos for when you really need them – like when you're on a plane or commuting", combined with an additional service: YouTube Music Premium.

The second scenario marks an interesting evolution. In this configuration, it is the content providers of the media who are given the opportunity to offer a subscription model to their own followers. Hence, the subscription model is mediated by the influencers and the media itself takes a small cut of the subscription fee, the model chosen by TikTok and Instagram. Besides creating a regular revenue stream for creators and influencers, the subscription model allows creators and users to develop a sense of community – which is lost when we talk about the audience – by providing additional and exclusive content. The main benefit is to bypass the algorithm which no longer wedges itself between users and influencers. These recent developments are extremely interesting, as they mitigate the traditional revenue models of social platforms.

A Final Consideration

Communication Apps like WhatsApp are finally starting to develop interesting business models. The reason why Facebook acquired WhatsApp for $19B in 2014 was that WhatsApp was becoming a threat as a substitute, as Facebook users (especially younger ones) were migrating to the communication app for their one-to-one and one-to-many interactions – no one knew how Facebook could one day recoup its investment. Before its acquisition, WhatsApp too had a subscription model. It cost $1 to download and then $1 a year going forward. Shortly afterwards, the parent company Facebook removed the subscription. WhatsApp now remains permanently free. It serves as a consumer service/communication platform where consumers communicate with businesses. WhatsApp makes money through its Business API product. It charges companies anywhere between $0.05 and $0.90 for every message that is answered after 24 h. WhatsApp's revenue in 2021 was $86.15 billion.

All the above examples constitute relatively new ways of making money. All these new models share the fact that they depart from the traditional advertising/data/audience revenue model. They may constitute the future of social platform revenue if such revenue can be sustainably integrated into a viable business ecosystem.

6 Unlocking the Sharing Economy: Scaling Trust with Digital

Tim Berners-Lee, the father of the World Wide Web, once said, "The original idea of the web was that it should be a collaborative space where you can communicate through sharing information". The vision was to develop an information distribution channel–the Internet– facilitating communication and enlarging the collaborative space. In a very real sense, the sharing economy glorifies why the Internet was created in the first place.

6.1 A Disruptive Phenomenon

As its name suggests, the notion of ownership is not important in the Sharing Economy. Instead, the focus is on the usage and the utility derived from the consumption of a good or service. This is often illustrated by the expression: "I don't need a drill. I need a hole in the wall". So, while a DIY enthusiast will buy a drill they can use repeatedly, why buy a drill at all, if you rarely do small household jobs? Wouldn't it be better if one could borrow or rent the drill and/or use a service that will satisfy his/her need– i.e., make the hole in the wall, or better yet, hang the picture on the wall (regardless of the method)?

At present, we are already used to renting cars and accommodation on-the-go. Extending this idea to other areas makes sense since the owner of a good or service can earn money from it when he/she is not using it. So, you could make a parking space you don't use available to others. This is what Parkpnp is enticing you to do: "Did you know that 1 in every 10 cars which drives past your home is looking for somewhere to park? Why not put your driveway to work while you kick back and enjoy benefits of up to €2,000 a year?"[1] Digital technologies make it possible to connect owners of such goods and services with those who need them.

However, let us not get ahead of ourselves and first understand the evolution of the sharing economy. The sharing economy began with giving, sharing, and swapping *things*–on websites like Craigslist, on which people posted classified advertisements for the items they wanted to get rid of and possibly earn some money. The benefit was that others could get those items at a cheaper rate (or sometimes free). Facebook Marketplace is one of the recent examples of this model.

The next phase of the sharing economy evolution was in sharing *space* –living space or space in your car. Airbnb used this model for the living space to become one of the biggest players in the sharing economy. In just 10 years of its inception, it became the world's largest accommodation provider. Though owning no real

---

1 https://parkpnp.com/ie/rent-your-parking-space as accessed on May 23, 2022.

estate, it lists more accommodation on its website than the Hilton and Marriott chains have rooms in their hotels after decades of doing business. The goal was not to create a marketplace where there is change of ownership but to match buyers and sellers. So, in the case of Airbnb, all accommodation remains the property of the host, there is just a "temporal rental" of an asset facilitated by Airbnb. BlaBlaCar is another example of the same model applied to ridesharing.

The sharing economy further evolved to encompass those who, for instance, "needed a drill but lacked the knowledge or training to use one". This was the genesis of the "service economy" that saw the emergence of sites like TaskRabbit or Fiverr where people posted small jobs, they needed doing and small service providers with relevant skills offered their service at low prices.

Thereafter came a more on-demand "gig economy", where people could establish themselves as independent workers, effectively creating their own jobs as Uber taxi drivers do. Irish grocery delivery company Buymie uses the gig economy principles to get pickers to shop on your behalf in your local Lidl or Dunnes Store and deliver your shopping list in less than an hour. By using existing shopping networks (actual shops) and flexible on-demand workforce, Buymie outcompetes on delivery time the traditional grocery websites (e.g., Tesco.ie) that support the cost of heavy infrastructure and logistics. Amazon Mechanical Turks is another, more recent example, in which Amazon uses the sharing economy model to perform what they call human intelligence tasks, such as writing product descriptions or identifying contents in an image/video.

The latest evolution is a move from services to highly skilled "expertise", with individuals sharing their knowledge for money. So, a business professor who offers to teach someone how to write a business plan in return for being taught another language by them would fall under the sharing economy, even though the deal is unbalanced, as one "expertise" would take much longer than the other to achieve. Gigster is another example of such a model that allows software developers a platform to offer their service for developing on-demand software.

However, there is no straightjacketing between the sharing and "non-sharing" (if one says so) economy as such.

For instance, would you consider an online learning platform, like Udemy, as part of the sharing economy? It provides a platform to the instructors and the students, respectively, to offer and access upskilling courses. While it is a platform, the content is simultaneously shared among multiple users. So, what classifies it better: digital platform or a sharing economy or perhaps both?

6.2 Seeing Through the Fog of Collaborative Economy

The notion of the sharing economy gets more confusing with the use of other terms such as collaborative consumption, collaborative economy, or peer economy, all of which are used interchangeably but have slightly different meanings. Because businesses create and exchange value differently through their diverse business models, the Collaborative Lab suggests there is a need to reach beyond current terminologies like "sharing economy", "peer economy", and "collaborative consumption". While we need to differentiate between these terms more precisely, these can be collectively thought of as falling under the overarching term, "collaborative economy".

A large element of the collaborative economy, of course, is collaborative consumption. It refers to the sharing, swapping, trading, or renting transactions that underpin collaborative consumption in the sharing economy. It may take the form of collaborative lifestyle, redistribution market, or product service systems. Under a collaborative lifestyle, resources are shared across a community. For instance, many cities have open book banks in public spaces, where anybody can put in a book or take one. Redistribution market refers to the situation when underused or unwanted goods are redistributed to those in need. For instance, Computer Aid, a charity organisation, collects unwanted computers from organisations and has sent those for use in more than hundred countries across the world. Finally, product service systems refer to the situation when people pay to access the service instead of owning the product. All major cities in the world now have some form of bicycle (e.g., Velib' in Paris or Dublin bikes) and car sharing systems (e.g., ShareNow in Germany or GoCar in Ireland), often in collaboration with the city councils.

Finally, the sharing economy could be defined more specifically as an economic model in which underutilised assets are shared, on a payment basis, with others. In contrast to the product service systems in which an external entity "owns" the shared resources (and takes care of maintenance, etc.), in the sharing economy, the emphasis is more on person-to-person redistribution. The resource is owned by an individual, who decides to share the underutilised resource, often in return for some money. The resource could include anything from sharing a car ride (say via BlaBlaCar), renting out a room to a traveller (say, via AirBnB), or/and exchanging knowledge (say, via Gigster). The companies only provide the platform to share the resource, while the resource ownership remains with the individual offering it.

While many businesses claim to be part of the sharing economy, not all meet the definition of a sharing economy business. For example, GoCar appears to be part of the sharing economy because it helps people share vehicles. Yet, the company owns these vehicles, and there is no peer-to-peer transaction. Hence, GoCar only ticks some of the boxes of the sharing economy. It is even more debatable for a company like Etsy. This platform is used by those looking to sell handcrafted goods, but since these products are made specifically to be sold, Etsy is in fact more accurately defined as a marketplace. Hence, there are different categories of sharing economy companies (see typology of business model hereafter).

As more goods and services are exchanged between peers, the sharing economy is expanding into new dimensions such as car and bicycle sharing, social lending, space rental and co-working, the swapping of books, baby goods, toys, clothing, etc.

The sharing economy is now extending to other traditional sectors too. In the energy industry, for instance, start-ups are looking to cut the carbon footprints of cities by rebalancing energy consumption between commercial and residential buildings, depending on the time of day. In many countries, consumers may install solar panels on the rooftop of their houses/offices and sell surplus electricity (i.e., electricity remaining after their use) to the grid.

6.3 Value Drivers Behind Sharing Economy

The sharing economy is propelled by four sets of drivers – technological, social, economic, and behavioural.

Technological Drivers

Digital technology is a crucial driver of the sharing economy. Idle capacity was always there; now, the technology has provided the means to share the information on idle capacity. Mobile technology has unlocked the potential of the network economy by facilitating peer-to-peer connections. Social networking and geolocation make it ever easier to find goods and services that meet consumers' needs. Powerful algorithms on the application platform make it easier to match the peers with complementary needs. Finally, peer-to-peer payment enables individuals to cover the last mile in the sharing economy.

Social Drivers

With the advent of social networks, there has been a rejuvenation of faith in the importance of the community (virtual and real) with a sense of togetherness, intimacy, and trust. In addition, the increasing resource burden on the cities has made the wider population receptive to the concept of sharing resources. The sharing economy redistributes power since consumers no longer need passively wait, as they did in the past for offers to be created for them. Now, thanks to crowdsourcing, consumers can participate in the creative process by helping fund the making of an offer that meets their needs. As consumers do not have to wait for a company or organisation to make what they want, this changes their relationships with the producers of goods and services. Moreover, there has been a disillusionment with the consumerist culture due to climate change, resulting in active citizenship in caring for environmental resources.

Economic Drivers

The sharing economy enables the creation of monetary value by using the idle capacity of resources. For instance, Airbnb hosts earn money by letting their idle space, which would be otherwise underutilised. The rising cost of living in cities has made the asset owners receptive to sharing the resource to reduce operational cost. For instance, ridesharing apps like BlaBlaCar allow car owners to reduce the cost of the travel they would have anyway made. The success of these sharing economy companies also has a ripple effect in terms of a steady supply of venture capitalists ready to invest in new sharing economy companies. Last but not the least, pervasive unemployment/underemployment post-recession make sharing and swapping increasingly attractive to those wanting to save money.

Behavioural Drivers

Apart from the technological, social, and economic factors, certain behavioural drivers have greatly influenced the adoption of the sharing economy. New app designs have made the interaction between peers–from search to match to payment– seamless. The ease of use and convenience attract and maintain the members on the sharing economy platform. There is also a desire for authentic experience – actual homes instead of hotel rooms or fellow travellers instead of a taxi driver–underlying the adoption of the sharing economy.

6.4 A Typology of Business Models Behind Digital Sharing

Based on the analysis of 32 companies that are part of sharing economy networks in the UK, Ireland, and Denmark, Trabucchi, Muzellec, and Ronteau (2019) classify digital sharing models across a two-by-two grid.[2] The business models may be classified on two crucial dimensions (Figure 6-A) – the novelty of the shared asset and the temporality of the transaction. The assets may be existing (pre-owned) or new. Similarly, the transaction could be temporary (e.g., rent) or permanent (ownership). Based on the two dimensions, four classes of digital sharing models may be identified.

---

2 Trabucchi, D., Muzellec, L., & Ronteau, S. (2019). Sharing Economy: Seeing through the Fog. Internet Research.

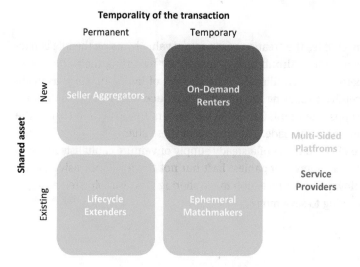

Figure 6-A: A Typology of Business Models Behind the Sharing Economy.
(Source: Trabucchi, Muzellec & Ronteau, 2019)

Lifecycle Extenders

Under this business model, peers sell existing goods permanently. These are the companies that extend the life cycle of used products by connecting the owners (who do not want the product anymore) to their future users. Peer-to-peer apps such as Craiglist, Done Deal, or ReSecond function as lifecycle extenders, when the users use these to buy and sell second-hand goods. This model is particularly popular in the case of sustainable fashion movement through websites such as Depop or Poshmark which facilitate the peer-to-peer sale of used fashion products. This model is not limited to individual customers. Rheaply, a company that provides a B2B service in the reuse of physical IT resources across companies, is another example.

Seller Aggregators

Under this business model, companies function as aggregators for newly created goods. For instance, apps like JustEat or Deliveroo aggregate the food providers. While these companies are better classified as platform businesses, they effectively share their delivery infrastructure with multiple partners.

On-Demand Renters

Under this business model, companies temporarily share their assets with a wide group of users. All businesses that rent cars or bikes come under this umbrella. Companies like Hertz or Europcar manage a vehicle fleet that could be temporarily rented by the customers. While the companies take care of the insurance and maintenance, the customers use the resource on a need basis. As discussed in the first section, on-demand renters are an example of collaborative consumption.

Ephemeral Matchmakers

Ephemeral matchmakers are the best example of a sharing economy model. Under this business model, companies function as a platform to enable temporary transactions between peers–those who own underutilised assets and those who wish to use them. This is the most popular model for sharing accommodation (AirBnB, HomeStay, Vrumi) and commuting (BlaBlaCar, Uber, Lyft). Since both parties are often individuals (aided by the digital platform), ephemeral matchmakers are closest to the concept of the sharing economy.

Irrespective of the classification, digital sharing companies often involve sharing of resources between strangers. This is where trust and reputation come into the picture. This is discussed in the next section.

6.5 Lemons Problem and Online Trust

To be successful, sharing economy companies need to overcome two key issues. They need to provide assurance to the participants concerning the quality and reliability of the product/service offered (*lemons problem*) and the integrity of the other participants, as well as of the digital transactions themselves (*online trust*).

Lemons Problem

Much before the advent of the online sharing economy, Nobel laureate George A. Akerlof discussed the issue of trust and information asymmetry in his 1970 paper "The Market for 'Lemons': Quality Uncertainty and the Market Mechanism". Akerlof argued that in such markets, usually, the sellers have more information on the product (e.g., a used car) than the buyers. Traditionally, the buyers did not have any mechanism to determine the authenticity of the information provided in such markets. This effectively drives the prices of the goods (lemons) down since buyers would not want to take a risk. With time, this phenomenon (known as the lemons problem) drives high-quality goods away from the market, inundating it with inferior quality goods.

Since the lemons problem emerges from information asymmetry, a key task for the sharing economy platforms is to facilitate information exchange to build trust and reputation. In the sharing economy, success depends on a company's ability to build trust among strangers, which means continually monitoring online reputation, right from the beginning. Sharing economy platforms like Airbnb or BlaBlaCar connect the two sides of a business that are not otherwise connected. In fact, it is the main reason they come to such a platform. Developing and maintaining trust is a result of recurring transactions in traditional businesses. However, due to the temporary nature of the transactions, the two entities seldom engage in repeated transactions in the sharing economy. Thus, ensuring trust between the two sides becomes a concern and a key requirement for an ephemeral matchmaker.

Online Trust and Reputational Mechanisms

As with other platforms, the primary challenge for sharing economy platforms is how to connect those who "have" with those who "need". And even though we are already accustomed to sharing, this often means overcoming resistance to new experiences. So, while parents, for instance, often exchange used baby clothes with others in their network of friends and family, doing this with strangers with whom you do not have an interpersonal relationship extends the concept of community into another area entirely.

When it comes to inspiring sufficient trust to make participants willing to interact with strangers in ways they would normally reserve for family and friends, sharing economy platforms face issues similar to those of other multi-sided platforms–how to attract both sides of the platform and encourage them to return. There are three ways in which sharing economy platforms can measure and manage trust – i.e., trust in other network participants, trust in the value exchanged, and trust in the platform.

Certain reputational mechanisms play a key role in ensuring trust between the buyers and the sellers and overall trust in the platform. Sharing economy platforms use at least three reputational mechanisms – profile, secure messaging, and reviews – that contribute to overcoming biases and reducing the anxiety of interacting with strangers. The majority of the sharing economy players encourage the users to build a complete profile (e.g., a driver on BlaBlaCar or a host on AirBnB) on their platform. A typical user profile on such sharing economy platforms includes information such as name, photograph, age, gender, and preferably social media handles. To ensure that the participants are trustworthy, BlaBlaCar has developed a framework for trust conditions called DREAMS. The framework outlines the key tools to build trust in online communities:

- **Declared** – Declared identity including name, photo, and bio.
- **Rated** – Peer-to-peer ratings based on members' prior rideshares.
- **Engaged** – Financial commitment to the journey through pre-payment service.
- **Activity** – Last-seen date or response rate, providing information on a member's frequency of activity, and level of responsiveness.
- **Moderated** – Content exchanged by members moderated and verified by the platform.
- **Social** – Existing online social identity (Facebook or LinkedIn) connected with profiles.

All sharing economy platforms will use similar forms of checking mechanisms to improve online trust for participants. They also enable secure messaging among users within their platform. Secure messaging provides a way of continuous communication and coordination, helping in building trust and maintaining the history of their communication on the same platform. All platforms provide rating and review mechanisms that allow other users who have availed of the service to rate the trustworthiness and reliability of another user and/or the quality of the offerings. Research suggests that textual reviews and the rating system are the strongest reputational mechanisms on sharing economy platforms. Customers can view the ratings and reviews before finalising a transaction.

While reputational mechanisms like profile and review help in building trust in the platform and the users, the crucial question of ensuring trust in the value exchanged remains. In planning the planning of the sharing economy platform, a company must work out not only how to inspire trust but also how it can make sharing and swapping transactions more efficient for all. This means those developing sharing economy platforms must consider the products involved in transactions and how they can provide a structure to facilitate interactions between those who have and those who need them. They must also think about the service offered as a whole—in other words, what will be the core interaction facilitated by the platform?

In this, the data collected and monitored as well as the reviews generated by the participants about the products and contents, they find on the platform are both crucial. For instance, efficient algorithms are designed that match the users (those who have and those who need) in an optimal way. Basic changes in the user interface, such as providing shortcuts for most used options, or options to filter/sort, go a long way to reduce friction and add value for the users. Similarly, most sharing economy platforms have integrated digital wallets into their applications so that the user remains within the system.

In the long run, however, trust in the platform also comes into the picture. Such trust-building ability effectively determines a sharing economy platform's capacity to scale. As a company matures, it must also determine how to extract more value from its community. For instance, AirBnB builds on the trust ecosystem through its "superhost program", with hosts who consistently provide an exceptional level of service.

Superhosts get benefits in the form of being featured on the platform, attracting more guests, and receiving additional bonuses from the platform. BlaBlaCar has a similar programme where their most active drivers are recognised as Ambassadors, who get featured on the platform and receive special benefits such as availing car-as-a-service with their partners like Opel and ALD.

However, the sharing economy platform needs to be careful in exploiting its user data. One area that significantly affects trust is the conditions of use of customer data. If customers feel, for instance, they are being asked for too much information, or worry about what will be done with their details, they will lose trust in the platform and use it less. For example, parents on baby clothes swapping platforms who provide information about their child's age, gender, and other details may find it objectionable if the company uses their profile to advertise baby products to them. So, issues of trust may stem not just from concerns over the safety of the transactions but also from how data is exploited by a platform.

6.6 Key Takeaways and Further Considerations

1. Sharing economy is a collaborative economic model in which users share their underutilised (idle) assets with others on a payment basis.
2. Most sharing economy services are ephemeral matchmakers who facilitate the transaction based on matching those who have with those who need.
3. Online trust and reputation play a crucial role in the sharing economy. User profiles and review/ratings are the most effective reputation- and trust-building mechanisms in sharing economy platforms.

Market Configurations that suit the Sharing Economy

When starting a sharing economy business, entrepreneurs must primarily consider the liquidity of the assets. In other words, are these goods or services easy to share? For example, a parking space in a secure apartment block might not be shareable if the residents object to outsiders having access to the building. However, there are often solutions to problems like this, thanks to the Internet of Things, which, in this instance, could provide a temporary remote key to the garage.

The next thing to consider is an asset with a high idling capacity, one that is used only infrequently (Figure 6-B). So, if someone owns a surfboard but uses it only once a month, they could rent it out for 30 other days. They would have to accept the possibility of the board being damaged and requiring replacement now and then.

The sharing economy may work well for the items for which the cost of ownership is high. It can make generally hard-to-access items like luxury goods more available. Through Airbnb, travellers can rent a luxury home in a desirable location

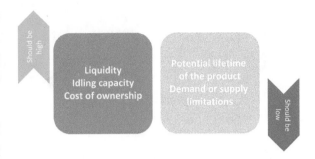

Figure 6-B: Characteristics of the Value Proposition in the Context of Sharing Economy.

at a lower price than if they booked a luxury hotel directly or through a letting agent.

In some cases, goods that quickly become obsolete are also good for sharing or swapping. Why purchase new baby clothes when they are only needed for a short time? Share them instead. In fact, in many cultures across the world (especially in Asia and Africa), it is customary for friends and family to gift old baby clothes when a baby is born.

The sharing economy also works well for assets that have low demand or supply limitations or the value of which increases when shared (e.g., travel experience or professional tips).

Part 3: **Capturing (and Locking) the Value: How Is Value Captured?**

Sustainability

7 Brokerage Model: Scaling with Fees on Marketplaces?

Commission fees are considered as the most developed and even sometimes successful model to capture value in marketplaces. Sometimes called "transaction fees", "take rate", or "rake" or "service fees", commissions are capable of minimising frictions in marketplaces. Transaction fees can be adjusted to attract both sides of the marketplace and solve the mutual baiting issues. This mode of value capture presents the advantage of exponential profit growth when scaling, provided variable costs are kept under control. Using AirBnB as a central case throughout this chapter enables us to analyse and illustrate the benefits and challenges associated with this value capture mechanism.

7.1 Why are Transaction Fees so Developed?

An internet transaction is the sale or purchase of goods or services, whether between businesses, households, individuals, governments, and other public or private organisations, conducted over the internet. In 2020, over two billion people purchased goods or services online, and during the same year, e-retail sales surpassed $4.2 trillion worldwide. Those transactions generate fees which may be visible or invisible to the users. This is the case of marketplaces like Airbnb, Amazon, Apple Store, Blablacar, Etsy, Uber, Zalando, and so on. If transaction fees are not the sole way to charge participants and customers, they are among the most dominant pricing mechanisms–namely the type of value capture behind the business model– at work in marketplace configurations. A recent study pointed out[1] that more than 50% of the "100 best performing marketplaces in 2021" take a cut out of the transactions they process.

The transactional business model can be considered a taken-for-granted marketplace model whereby two sides (i.e., buyers and sellers) engage in a transaction and thus generate revenue for the marketplace provider. The value is captured by charging one or both sides a service fee, a commission fee, sometimes called a "rake", on each successful transaction.

The "rake" analogy is interesting, as it reveals why this pricing tactic spreads among marketplaces. As Bill Gurley explained, "In a casino, the term 'rake' refers to the commission that the house earns for operating a poker game. With each hand, a small percentage of the pot is scraped off by the dealer, which in essence becomes the 'revenue' for the casino". Like a casino, a marketplace provider

---

1 See ShareTribe insights accessed in May 2022.

creates the conditions by which all the participants– at least a seller-side and a buyer-side– want to interact and transact. For their effort and just like the dealer in a casino, these providers capture a little bit (e.g., the commission) of the revenue passing through (e.g., the transaction).

Let us take Airbnb as an example. Originally named AirBed&Breakfast, this business was presented in 2008 and their pitch deck got viral and influenced numerous upcoming entrepreneurs.[2] Behind their well-known solution – "a web platform where users can rent out their space to host travellers" – founders stated simply their business model as such: "we take a 10% commission on each transaction". Let's assume that one transaction corresponds on average to three nights for $70 per night – or $210 – the company will take a $21 commission per transaction. Based on an estimated 10.6 million transactions in the next 3 years, AirBed&Breakfast could achieve more than $200 million in revenue–not bad for a startup with a relatively limited upfront investment – i.e., contrary to a traditional hotel chain, it does not need to pay for the building of the actual offering (e.g., hotels and hotel rooms). As we will see later, the "business model" is a bit more complex, but what can we learn from that example?

At the Essence of Two-Sided Markets

Theorized by French economists, the Nobel laureates Jean Tirole and Jean-Charles Rochet, two-sided markets are at the foundations of digital platforms, as presented earlier. They refer to a situation in which two distinct user groups (sides) are interdependent on interaction (buying and selling for example). To enhance network effects, an intermediary– the platform provider– will have to create favourable conditions to remove frictions to meet, interact, and hopefully transact. This intermediary transactional platform is accordingly supposed to function as a facilitator – often called a matchmaker – to foster the willingness of the sides to meet and transact.

Thus, charging a fee for each transaction is supposed to support the efficiency of the intermediation provided, as it will take a small commission on the effective transactions performed. Individually, each commission represents an acceptable and small compensation for the effective matchmaking (e.g., a 10% compensation for securing the transaction between a host and a traveller for AirBed&Breakfast). But on a large scale, these small commissions can represent a huge revenue stream, once the provider reaches a significant market share (e.g., $200 million in expected revenue from 2008 to 2011 for AirBed&Breakfast).

---

2 See this BusinessInsider Blog Article published on March 28, 2015 – accessed in May 2022.

As the platforms' key attribute is to remove frictions in the matching and inter-action of two sides, it is essential that the pricing mechanism does not reintroduce such frictions.

Capturing Value from a Frictionless Transaction and Brokerage Model

Instead of buying products and reselling them, brokers function as an intermediary or third-party who brings sides together and removes the friction in transacting. The goal of the broker is to hopefully become the "one-stop shop" for buyers; and the place to be listed for sellers. So, to justify the 10% commission fee, we need to understand how the job is performed by the web platform. In the example of Air-Bed&Breakfast, the platform provides three key features for travellers:
- Travellers can search by city and curate the listing according to filters.
- They can review listings: each reference can be described according to a text, pictures, a functional description, and reviews from previous travellers – which play a key role in continuously updating the description of each listing.
- They can book directly on the web platform, whether or not the currency of the host and the traveller is the same. The website secures the transaction for both participants, as it ensures the role of a bank in settling the transaction.

This last attribute of the process is key for AirBed&Breakfast. If it did not control the flow of money, it would not be able to ensure that both participants pay a commission.

LeBonCoin, on the other hand, is a classified ads website based on free service for individuals and the matching of local supply and demand. In this model, buyers and sellers are put in contact through the website but the money flows directly from buyers to sellers without the intermediation of LeBonCoin. In this case, it is not possible to secure the conditions for a commission. That explains why LeBonCoin prefers to value the exposure from the audience to advertisers and function as a third-party subsidy business model that we will discuss in Chapter 8 on free-based business models.

Providing enough value for participants is key to sustaining a commission model. If the participants can interact directly – especially for the payment – then the platform may lose its pivotal role in the brokerage ecosystem model. In our ex-ample, AirBed&Breakfast re-intermediated the market with transactional ease of payment combined with trust mechanisms (ratings of hosts, travellers and offer-ings). Airbed&Breakfast acts as "insurance" for both parties and as such, justifies the commission fee.

A One-Fits-All Pricing Strategy for Marketplaces?

As stated by ShareTribe in their survey,[3] commission fees are dominant for rental marketplaces and marketplaces selling physical goods. Whereas for the other kind of marketplaces, such as for digital goods and contents, or service, and delivery marketplaces, ShareTribe notes "a spread of successful revenue models" including subscription, freemium and lead fees, and other kinds.

As explained earlier for rental services, such as Airbnb, the trust issues justify the brokerage model. For marketplaces selling physical goods (such as Amazon for example), the service fees need to encompass the shipping process where the e-commerce will release to the seller the details for the shipping to the buyer, the seller performing the delivery directly. Thus, the platform provider is locking in the seller by mastering the customer relationship management, justifying and securing the commission. If a transaction is recurring between the same buyer and seller for the same good or rental, then buyers and sellers will be tempted to bypass the marketplace.

For digital goods and contents, value capture may also be different. Sometimes, the dominance of the platforms makes it possible to charge larger fees, as much as 30%, as in the case of Apple. The mimetic movement for spreading the commission fees from music to applications was successful, as it was well-adopted by the eco-system of stakeholders. Whatever the nature of the transaction, the effects were a quick scale of catalogues and consequently, a solid revenue for the platform providers as the number of transactions grows and the platform reaches a dominant position. The example of Apple is developed hereafter, concerning two different services: iTunes and App. Store.

Apple iTunes vs. Apple AppStore
Released in 2002, iTunes rapidly became an extremely popular marketplace for buying music to be downloaded on an iPod (a portable media player) released by Apple by late 2001. At this time, the music industry was still dominated by CDs. Thus, purchasing music as a physical good was the dominant model. To enhance the move to digital, Apple engineered an interesting business model for iTunes. On the one side, we find the copyright owners – major labels and distributors such as Universal, Warner, and EMI, with a dominant position in the industry. At 10 to 15€ per copy, they were benefitting from the CD format. The challenge for Apple with iTunes was therefore to convince them to disseminate electronic copies of their catalogues without a risk of music piracy. Then Apple needed to change consumers' habits to wean them away from CDs to purchasing digital copies. In that context, Apple fixed the price for every single to be sold on Apple iTunes at 0.99€ per song. A price per song was appealing to the listener, who did not need to buy a full album. This pricing was also considered fair and beneficial to the owners, as on average, an album comprised 12 to 15 songs – thus, the price of an album would be comparable, as Apple promised to integrate a Digital Right Management to secure each copy sold online exclusively through the Apple iTunes platform. On the volume of sales, Apple split the

---

3 See ShareTribe insights accessed in May 2022.

revenue generated with Majors on a 30/70 split agreement: Apple's retaining a commission fee of 30% of the revenue was justified by the costs of distribution (storage, security of digital content and platform, marketing, and payment costs). iTunes was an enormous success for many years and an accelerator of progress from an analogic industry to a digital music industry, opening up avenues for streaming platforms.

Several years later, in 2007, Apple introduced the first iPhone, replicating the model it had already tested with iTunes with some slight differences. Along with the iPhone, the AppStore was launched as a marketplace. iPhone owners could browse and download approved apps developed for iOS (the operating system embedded in iPhones). App developers could access Apple iOS SDK (i.e., the Software Development Kit) and access all iPhone customers if they respected Apple's conditions of sales and use.

Yet, contrary to the iTunes business model, this time, Apple did not fix the price of Applications, due to the competitive conditions of the application industry. Unlike the music industry, the application development sector is highly competitive, the players numerous and fragmented. Accordingly, the conditions are very competitive to ensure that the laws of pure and perfect competition are fulfilled and accessible pricing for the buyers (iPhone owners) is possible – to the extreme, nowadays, we observe that a large majority of Apps are offered for free.

Reproducing a "fair pricing brokerage model", Apple let developers fix the price of their apps and split the revenue under the 30/70 rule: 70% of revenues for developers for paid apps and in-app purchases and 30% for Apple to cover service fees. Again, it was a tremendous success for Apple. It permitted Apple to quickly scale the catalogue of applications developed in the iOS ecosystem, faster than it could have taken for Apple to develop on its own all the applications available in its closed ecosystem.

Finally, for delivery services, the platform provider must intermediate three sides (e.g., restaurants, customers, and riders for Deliveroo or Uber Eat) and conditions to transact can be made complex with other kinds of pricing strategies.

If the mechanism for "commission fees" appears simple in principle, its practical application may be more complex.

7.2 Who is Willing to Pay the Bill?

Behind the lure of scaling of revenues, the way service fees and commission fees are split among sides plays a vital role in the success or failure of marketplaces. Traditionally, the pricing level should be directly related to the consumer's willingness to pay. For the brokerage model, the fees need to be paid by one side or both sides proportionally to their willingness to use the service.

Coming back to AirBnB, the initial and symbolic 10% commission on each transaction evolved over time. Today, the fees ranging between 7 to 15% are supported by the traveller-side (guests) (according to Airbnb, under 14.2% in most cases), whereas hosts contribute 3% from their side. The communicated "10% on average" may end up being much more (at least for the platform), as the cost may be supported by both sides (see Figure 7-A).

airbnb's conditions of service:	transaction value used for the example
3% on the host side	3 nights @ $100 per night = $300
14,2% on the guest side*	
*average commissions observed by Airbnb	

What the traveller (guest) will see and pay:

$100 x 3 nights	$300
Cleaning fees	$30
Service fees	$42,60
Lodging taxes*	$33
Total	**$405,60**

*(10% of nightly rate + fees)

airbnb commission on transaction

Guest service fees	$42,60
Host service fees	$9,90
Total	$52,50

the total represents 17,53% of the $300 transaction

What the host (guest) will receive after the stay:

100 € x 3 nights	$300
Cleaning fees	$30
Service fees (3%)	-$9,9
Total	$320,1

airbnb will also collect lodging taxes
and pay once a year each local authorities

airbnb collects the payment and transfers it to the
host 24 hours after the start of the stay

Figure 7-A: Breakdown of a Typical Transaction on Airbnb.
(Example based on dummy data)

Avoiding the Chicken and Egg Issues with Fees

Defining the billing process requires the platform providers to perfectly know the characteristics of the markets (sides) they are intermediating.

Then, different options are accessible for the platform provider to capture the value of the interaction enhanced: charging one side or splitting the commission between sides.

In the design of the pricing strategy, the challenge here is not to introduce frictions with applicable fees to join the platform and trade (transact). Pricing is part of the marketing mix, along with products and services, communication, and UX on the platform, and must bring liquidity and transparency for the participants, to avoid the chicken and egg issue.[4]

Pricing will play a role in the mutual baiting problem. Subscription fees or listing fees, for example, should not represent a potential obstacle to joining.

At the nascent stage of a marketplace, the platform is "supply constrained": No listing of restaurants on a food delivery app, no drivers available on a taxi app, and no hosts on a rental app will make it impossible to attract potential customers on the other side. Hence, the platform provider may have to provide its services on both sides for low fees or no fees.

---

4 See Chapter 2.

To charge the supply side, platform providers need to know their dependence on the trading service provided. In the case of Airbnb, hosts have an alternative in the form of real estate agents, who traditionally play the role of brokers but with a more limited audience. Usually, they take a 4% commission per month to manage the rentals for hosts. Positioning Airbnb just under this competitive price (3%) was a necessity to be attractive. Moreover, beyond the access to a larger audience of potential guests, the service provided by Airbnb permits benefiting from a landing page and back-office tools (calendar to manage availabilities, seasonal pricing management tool, message interface, smart pricing suggestions, a third-party insurance system, secured payment logistics, etc.) to position their ads on the Internet. Thus, the conditions of fees are made frictionless and worth the investment, as they extend opportunities for maximising the property occupancy rate.

In the initial phase of development, very few platforms are "demand constrained". Accordingly, a large part of the marketing effort is oriented towards the buyer side to invite them to scroll and search for the perfect good or service to transact. The challenge here is at the check-out, where service fees listed beyond the raw price of the transaction can introduce a barrier to an effective transaction.

Here, the psychological price acceptable to the buyer is a combination of several elements relative to the nature of transactions (e.g., including speed shipping for eCommerce platforms, trust mechanisms in rental services, easiness of booking and payment for a taxi app) and the value perceived for the brokerage activity performed.

The fee mechanisms along the way of scaling will gradually become more complex. Data analytics help the platform provider to complexify the conditions of commissions: a split changing over time, differentiated segmentation based on the level of usage-based or based on loyalty, etc. The provider can test different alternatives with the hope of securing revenues and being less dependent on the Gross Merchandise Volume growth rate.

7.3 Pricing: The Influence of Competition and Cost

Defining the optimal level of commissions and their split among sides is an equilibrium exercise. Several contracting forces will determine the optimal price.

A Competitive Pressure

Multihoming is an established practice on the Internet. It consists of registering with several services offering similar solutions. For example, many Internet users subscribe to different cloud services such as Google Drive, One Drive (Microsoft), DropBox, or Apple iCloud. The same exists for buyers and sellers on marketplaces.

A seller will list its products on Amazon, eBay, maybe Etsy, and potentially its own eShop powered by Shopify. A traveller may search and review on Airbnb, Booking.com, and Tripadvisor, while a host may propose rooms via Airbnb, Homelidays, and Booking.com. Accordingly, fees are subject to competitive pressure, and whatever is the value perceived, these tend to lower commissions. Commoditisation is a huge danger for all marketplaces—a point where participants do not really see the differentiated value from one marketplace to another. In such a situation, platform providers enter a "red ocean situation", as described by Kim and Maubourgne, authors of the bestseller *Blue Ocean Strategy*. In this situation, competition is typically fierce, and all companies are fighting to solve the same problem or meet the same need; very often the only way to gain a percentage of market share is to battle prices.

Fees can be a differentiator in attracting and reducing switching costs. Conversely, transaction fees alone are less effective in retaining customers. Hence, it is important to see the "lock-in effect" of a pricing strategy such as for the non-financial attributes of the platform. The more a participant engages (creating an account, uploading content, searching, connecting often, transacting often, etc.), the more (s)he is locked into the service. Customers are eventually locked into a vendor's world of products and services. Switching to another vendor is not possible without incurring substantial additional costs. Apple locks-in users of its Macbook, iPhone, and iPad because they share a common operating system, which makes syncing data between each device very easy and syncing with third-party systems such as Android rather inconvenient or impossible. Another way to lock in users is to perform the razor and blade strategy. This strategy, whose name can be traced to Gillette's practice of charging a low attractive price for the razor and higher price for blades, is now used in other industries too. Canon, for example, takes advantage of digital technology to sell ink printers at fair prices and charges very high prices for replacement ink cartridges, which are automatically ordered through the Internet, once the ink runs low.

Covering the Platform Costs

To enter a market (e.g., e-commerce, taxi apps, digital goods marketplaces, and delivery apps), insurgents engage in a "blitzscaling strategy"[5] with the hope of getting over the crowd before running out of cash. This strategy allows them to rationalise their pricing strategy according to the expectations of investors to see the accrual of profits. What is at stake here? The Profit Formula is quite simple (see Figure 7-B).

---

5 As defined by Reid Hoffman and Chris Yeh in their book: 'Blitzscaling: The Lightning-Fast Path to Building Massively Valuable Companies', Currency, 2018.

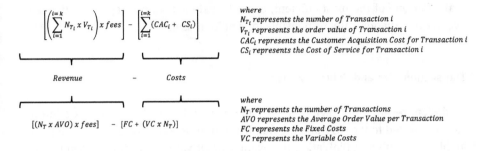

$$\left[\left(\sum_{i=1}^{i=k} N_{T_i} \times V_{T_i}\right) \times fees\right] - \left[\sum_{i=1}^{i=k}(CAC_i + CS_i)\right]$$

where
N_{T_i} *represents the number of Transaction i*
V_{T_i} *represents the order value of Transaction i*
CAC_i *represents the Customer Acquisition Cost for Transaction i*
CS_i *represents the Cost of Service for Transaction i*

$\underbrace{\qquad\qquad}_{Revenue}$ — $\underbrace{\qquad\qquad}_{Costs}$

$$[(N_T \times AVO) \times fees] \quad - \quad [FC + (VC \times N_T)]$$

where
N_T *represents the number of Transactions*
AVO *represents the Average Order Value per Transaction*
FC *represents the Fixed Costs*
VC *represents the Variable Costs*

Figure 7-B: Simplified Profit Formula for a Brokerage Model.
(Adapted from our fictional example)

As we can see in the simplified profit formula for a brokerage model:
- options to increase revenue rely on the left side of the formula:
    - increasing the Number of Transactions (N_T) and/or
    - increasing the Average Order Value (AOV) per Transaction and/or
    - increasing fees
- whereas, to improve profits, you can also (maybe even need) to maintain costs:
    - limit Fixed Costs (FC) and reduce variable costs (VC)
    - reduce the Customer Acquisition Costs (CAC), play on word of mouth and referrals, and develop inbound marketing instead of outbound marketing tactics.
    - reduce the Cost of Service (CS), by playing on automation of processes to avoid a trader behind each transaction.

The major issue is that a large part of FC is supported at the beginning of the entrepreneurial journey (e.g., development of the platform) and CAC and CS are higher at the beginning due to a lack of efficiency in operations (economy of scope and experience). Sustaining and winning the battle of establishing the positioning require a lot of working capital and the backing of investors. Amazon waited till 2001 to generate its first operating profits. It took 16 years for its profits to cover its peak cumulative losses of $3 billion. Equally, it took 8 years for BlaBlaCar to generate its first profits. The tipping point of revenues and breakeven is hard to find, and it requires considerable energy for entrepreneurs to financially achieve the potential of network effects in their markets. Nowadays, BlaBlaCar represents a community of more than 100 million users (drivers and passengers) worldwide.

In the UK, BlaBlaCar fees are between £2 and £9 depending on the price of the ride. This means that the margins are low and could be easily eaten up if VC get out of control. To sustain profitability, BlaBlaCar relies on automation. About 98% of transactions are effective and without incident. Still, customer service represents one-seventh of its workforce (700 employees). This makes customer service at

BlaBlaCar one of the most efficient, as each customer service representative is on average and theoretically responsible for a million users!

Transaction Size and Volume Matter

By design, revenues for digital brokers and marketplaces adopting fees are intrinsically correlated to the AOV and the number of transactions. To continue with the example of Airbnb and BlaBlaCar, the average order value is no comparison between the two companies. Airbnb generates an average transaction of more than $200: users book for a weekend (two nights) or a week (five nights) for an average cost per night of $70 initially but rising continuously since then. The carpooling service promoted by BlaBlaCar generates an average transaction of 13€. BlaBlacar does not charge fees to drivers who will get "the exact amount they set when offering a ride" – as pointed out in BlaBlaCar conditions of sale. For most markets, BlaBlaCar charges between 0 and 30% according to the order value with a minimum of 1€. Thus, each transaction on BlaBlaCar generates on average 2€ – which is 10 times lower than Airbnb commission fees or, put differently, BlaBlaCar needs 10 times more transactions to generate the same revenue. Nevertheless, the business architecture remains as complex and difficult to scale as previous developments demonstrated.

Entrepreneurs eager to develop a digital service and a viable business model need to consider a sustainable and scalable business model capable of generating recurrent revenue that will lead to profitability. It may not be viable immediately, as business models may evolve over time through trial and error. BlaBlaCar, which is present in 22 countries, tested different business models over time and geographical markets. Business models are organic and must evolve over time according to the characteristics of the markets and their participants–so too are the digital business models; and, among them, the brokerage model, which is enticing as it is simple and frictionless to scale and yet also needs to be tested and fine-tuned over time.

7.4 Key Takeaways and Further Considerations

1. Fees can be seen as a frictionless pricing strategy for digital platforms and marketplaces.
2. Fees should entice fluidity in the marketplace and reflect transparency.
3. The value of the brokerage activities justifies the value of the fees.
4. The pricing strategy and value capture mechanism should be adapted to different market configurations.

Airbnb: Fees are Moving, Does it Change the Business Model?

The pandemic has grounded travellers and business trips for the last two years: bad news for AirBnB. Research by the analysis website AirDNA showed bookings in some cities to have fallen by as much as 96%. But even before this, AirBnB had experienced some level of difficulty. For example, many voices on social media have criticised the balance between the price per night listed and the effective guest price paid per transaction, which can double with local taxes, cleaning fees, and of course, service fees.

In parallel, Airbnb revised its pricing policy in 2020 with the "Airbnb Simplified Pricing". This is what the Airbnb website says:[6]

> Historically, Airbnb has had a single fee structure for all hosts, in which a service fee is charged to both the host (3%) and the guest (under 14.2% in most cases). Last year, based on feedback from many professional hosts, we launched a new fee option for software-connected hosts to remove the guest service fee and provide hosts with more control over their rates. This fee structure is known as Simplified Pricing.
>
> From December 7[th]2020, Simplified Pricing (15% host fee) will be the only available fee structure to all software-connected hosts on Airbnb globally (excludes US, Canada, Mexico, Uruguay, The Bahamas, Argentina, and Taiwan).

Airbnb claims that benefits are there, especially on the host side:

> This new service fee structure will allow you to have a simpler pricing strategy as you'll be able to set what the guests will pay. We'll also highlight the fact that there is no guest service fee added to your rates, making your listings more attractive to many guests. Hosts that have decided to switch and keep their prices competitive across channels have seen an overall increase in their bookings (~17%*).
> *Average observed bookings increase for hosts using host-only fee in Europe between November 2019 and February 2020. Actual results may vary for each host.

We tested with the previous example the consequences of the move in the pricing strategy (see Figure 7-C).

What do we see? Let's ask the following questions:

– Will hosts adjust their rates?
Probably yes. Airbnb proposes to host a "Software Provider" to ensure that hosts' earnings will not be impacted. But at the same time, Airbnb calls on its hosts to remain competitive. And for that, they developed a tool–"smart pricing" to provide advice to hosts on positioning their prices competitively according to seasonality and alternatives. Hence, we can assume that prices will appear higher for the guests in listings (negative impact) but with a pleasant surprise at not having to pay service fees upon check-out (positive impact).

---

6 See dedicated page on Airbnb website consulted in May 2022.

airbnb's old conditions of service:	airbnb's new conditions of service*:
3% on the host side	15% on the host side
14,2% on the guest side*	0% on the guest side
*average commission estimated by Airbnb	*in the United States, Canada, the Bahamas, Mexico, Argentina, Taiwan, or Uruguay

transaction value used for the example*
3 nights @ $100 per night = $300
* amount expected for the host and to maintain

What the host will receive after the stay:

$114,12* x 3 nights	$342,36
Cleaning fees	$34,27
Service fees	-$56,50
Total	$320,13

*To maintain its objective of $100 per night, the host will have
to adapt the pricing as follow:

$$\text{New base price} = \text{old base price} \times \frac{(1 - previous\ host\ fees)}{(1 - new\ host\ fees)}$$
$$= \text{old base price} \times \frac{(1-0,03)}{(1-0,15)}$$
$$= \text{old base price} \times 1,1412$$

What the traveller (guest) will see and pay:

$114,2 x 3 nights	$342,36
Cleaning fees	$34,27
Service fees	$0
Lodging taxes*	$34,20
Total	$410,83

*(10% of nightly rate + fees)

airbnb commission on transaction

Guest service fees	$00,00
Host service fees	$56,50
Total	$56,50

the total represents 16,5% of the $342,36 transaction
and 18,83% of the old value order ($300 transaction)

Figure 7-C: Example Based on the New Airbnb Simplified Pricing.

– If things do not change for Airbnb, why change?
In the example and based on our hypothesis that hosts will adjust their rates, we observe a jump from $52.50 to $56.50 for the commissions perceived by Airbnb, representing an increase of more than 7% of their commission per transaction.

Of course, it is slack, as potentially, the competitive pressures on hosts will limit the adjustments of rates. But Airbnb will generate higher revenues with that strategy.

– Can those adjustments change the business model?
Over the years, Airbnb has lost the community aspects that characterised it in its early days. Nowadays, many commentators feel that it is more of a nicely branded marketplace. Professional hosts have populated the website and have benefitted greatly from Airbnb as a distribution channel. The move in the pricing strategy can be seen as defending this community sense and differentiating pricing among participants on the host side. As Airbnb explicitly mentions, this move affects "software-connected hosts" – meaning professionals multihoming their listings and managing them with a channel manager. Accordingly, it is not a change in the business model but certainly a marketing re-orientation. Guests will not see these behind-the-scenes manoeuvres. Airbnb will increase its revenue with this apparent transparency for hosts, which in fact will induce opacity for guests and inflate the rates applicable on Airbnb.

8 The Magnitude of Subscription: Monetisation of "Everything-as-a-Service"

The world is moving from the ownership model to the subscription model – thanks to the adoption of a service-dominant logic in the firms. How digital is enhancing that? And what is the rationale for a subscription-based business model?

8.1 A Subscription Economy?

Subscription models are not new but can be extremely efficient as a competitive differentiator and value capture mechanism – Xerox provides a good example of how powerful and disruptive it can be (see box below). Apart from day-to-day needs such as newspapers or milk, car leasing is an excellent example of the subscription economy. Here, the car manufacturer's margins are not made on the sale of the car but generated from the finance plans involved in the leasing agreements or the maintenance fees. By requiring the user to have maintenance performed by the manufacturer's mechanic, annual service fees generate higher revenue for the company, while the user enjoys the assurance of a functioning car and a fixed budget free of repairs and maintenance. The effortless or worry-free principle partially explains the attraction of this mode of value exchange mechanism for users in a digital world.

The Birth of a Subscription Mindset
In the late 1950s, Haloid Xerox innovated with a disruptive and incredibly fast and efficient printer. With a capacity of 2,000 prints per day, the XEROX 914 had a serious competitive advantage over other printers available then. The main issue for Haloid Xerox was its price. Between 1947 and 1960, Haloid spent $75 million – twice its operational earnings – on xerography research.

To recoup the costs of developing this innovation, the printer would have to be sold close to eight times the price of a traditional printer. Not surprisingly, a top consulting company advised Xerox that at that price, "there is no market for such a printer". The solution was found with a shift in the value proposition: "companies do not need printers; they look for a printing service".

Instead of selling a product, Haloid Xerox designed an offer around service with an incentive subscription plan: $95/month for 2,000 prints per day (+2 cents/print outside the plan). This marketing shift was a success for the company, gaining a lot of traction on the market with companies rapidly consuming 2,000 prints a day.

Even if the financial results were not released by Haloid Xerox, the XEROX 914 is credited with the financial success of the company, which generated over $243 million of total operating revenues by 1965. More importantly, the subscription model radically transformed the printing industry.

The number of subscription-based digital business models has proliferated largely due to this new marketing approach – the service-dominant logic of the firm, which[1] describes service as the core purpose of exchange and how firms, customers, and other market actors co-create value through their mutual service interactions.

Digital contents/products are extremely well suited to the subscription logic. Music, movies, or software are dematerialised items that can be stored on servers and delivered through dedicated platforms. The increasing speed and bandwidth of the internet enable the existence and proliferation of streaming services such as Amazon Prime, Disney plus, and Netflix. The content is provided as a service and the user does not own the content as such. At the B2B level, cloud computing has heralded the era of subscription-based technology services such as Amazon web services, Microsoft Office 365, or Salesforce service cloud.

Consumers are now well accustomed to this model of value exchange. Some studies estimate that two-thirds of our monthly expenses are based on subscriptions (mobile plans, streaming services, leasing, Internet, electricity bill, bank services, etc.). For companies, a subscription is a good opportunity to present value-added assets before equity and liabilities on a balance sheet.

The Subscription Trade Association estimates that by 2019, 18% of all global payments (around $41 trillion) were recurring payments, or generated by subscription. It also predicts that around 75% of the organisations that are selling directly to consumers will offer subscription services by 2023.

> Subscription-based business models are at the core of the access economy. They rely on a shift from ownership to access by delivering products or services as long as the customer pays for it with recurring subscription fees (usually monthly or yearly). So saying, subscription-based business models rely on a simple recurring pricing mechanism to access a good or service.

8.2 "Everything"-as-a-Service

Underlying the subscription-based business models is the emergence of a service-dominant logic by the firms (Vargo & Lusch, 2004, 2008).

---

1 Often named S-D logic, service-dominant logic was largely conceptualized by Vargo and Lusch. See Vargo, S. L. & Lusch, R. F. (2004). The Four Service Marketing Myths: Remnants of a Goods-based, Manufacturing Model. *Journal of Service Research*, 6(4), 324–335; and Vargo, S. L. & Lusch, R. F. (2008). Service-Dominant Logic: Continuing the Evolution. *Journal of the Academy of Marketing Science*, 36(1), 1–10.

Service as the Dominant Basis for Exchange

The traditional demarcation of service and goods has become partially obsolete due to the servitisation of the economy, especially in developed economies. Owning an iPhone or MacBook is not just a question of buying a device. The device is just the entrance to an overall service experience. Consumers pay to benefit from the Apple ecosystem and access its service offerings.

Those who cannot afford the latest iPhone do not have to miss out if they lease one for an affordable monthly payment through a mobile operator like Sprint. Sprint, a mobile leasing service, does not make a profit on the handset in the short term but does so in the future. The company provides financial convenience that keeps its customers loyal in the long term. The same may be true even for "hard" goods such as cars, where after-sales services are equally important as the sales, not to mention additional services like financing and payment installments.

Accordingly, by adopting a subscription-based business model, companies extend their value proposition to a "bundle of products and services". The subscription plan removes economic friction in accessing and testing a user experience and locking in the customer in the service, as long as (s)he is satisfied.

Customer as Co-creator of Value

According to the service-dominant logic, customers are not only a receiver of value, but also essentially the co-creators of value. Vargo and Lusch (2008) argue that the firm does not create value by itself; it can only propose a value (value proposition) to interested parties. With a subscription plan and the monitoring of the user experience, companies can identify the value adopted by customers and the most relevant features in the service.

In this sense, customers select the attributes/features on:
- an active mode by adjusting their user experience according to the personalisation tools provided with the product and service.
- a passive mode by providing data on the most-consulted contents and recommendations automatically formulated, as they are not necessarily aware of being spied on.

The value is created when the consumers engage with the application to create, share, and consume content. Marvel Cinematic Universe or games such as Fortnite create such a huge value for the company primarily owing to their large and loyal fan base. The Lego Group has explicitly tapped the potential of customers as co-creators by inviting ideas from Lego enthusiasts and using those ideas in their offerings.

Value Creation as a Network Process

Vargo and Lusch (2008) observe that a service-dominant perspective is not dyadic (i.e., an exchange between the firm and the consumer). They argue that the process of value creation unfolds at multiple levels, involving multiple stakeholders. For instance, Amazon as a retailer creates value based on the work of the manufacturers, packaging facility, supply chain network, internet technology, and, most importantly, the substantial number of buyers and sellers present on the platform. Vargo and Lusch (2016) aver that the work of the enterprise is to integrate and transform various competencies into complex service arrangements valued by the end consumers. So, the servitisation of the economy goes with a more interconnected economy where complementors can interconnect easily through technological gateways (APIs and platforms) and extend progressively the value proposition which can be pushed forward. A perfect example is EVENTBRITE and Spectrum initiative[2] (App Marketplace). The ticketing company enhances the user experience for both sides (creators and consumers) by developing a third-party platform where other companies can plug in their services and technologies to add value. This is the birth of an ecosystem around a value proposition.

But how does the servitisation of the economy relate to the rise of the subscription economy? A good example is provided by the software industry.

From "Software as a Product" to "Software as a Service"

A few years ago, the majority of software needed to be installed on your device to be used with physical media (disk, CD, or DVD). This could be the Microsoft Office suite for your personal use or SAP enterprise systems to be used by your company. While the cost of a personal copy of Microsoft Office may not be much, installing multiple copies for all employees was a cost and source of "pain" for companies. The software-as-a-product generated frictions: on the provider side, the sold licence did not permit the lock-in of customers for a longer period beyond the next release; on the customer side, the purchase of a licence represented an important financial investment that would depreciate over time.

Software-as-a-service, commonly known as SaaS will change all this. As the name suggests, SaaS architecture allows software components to be delivered to clients through the internet. The user just needs an active internet connection and a working machine to access the functionality. Since the service is hosted and managed remotely by the vendor for several clients (resource pooling), it can be offered at the fraction of the cost of the in-house software installation and to a large number of users. The

---

2 See Eventbrite app marketplace consulted in May 2022.

client pays a subscription fee on a monthly or annual basis. Microsoft Office 365 is one such example of subscription-based SaaS.

Along with other innovations like infrastructure as a service and platform as a service, this phenomenon is commonly known as cloud computing. The majority of vendors now offer industrial software such as customer relationship management, supply chain management, enterprise resource planning, payroll management, and data centres as subscription-based cloud services. Gartner estimates[3] the worldwide cloud market to be $182.4 billion in 2018, which is expected to reach $354.6 billion by 2022, at a compounded annual growth rate of 12.6%. Thus, the entire software product and infrastructure industry have moved to a subscription-based service model in recent years.

In recent years, the sharing economy is also partially responsible for the momentum of subscription business models (see Chapter 6).

Pricing in Subscription Business Model

Potential disadvantages of the subscription-based business model relate to fixed costs and fixed prices. A subscription-based service incurs certain fixed costs irrespective of the number of subscriptions. Thus, companies need at least a certain number of users to cover their operational expenses. Fixed price means that even if customers were probably willing to pay more for a service, the service could not tap it. This means potential revenue opportunities are lost.

In the US, MoviePass is a perfect example of subscription-based pricing gone wrong. MoviePass was trying to establish itself as an intermediary between the cinema halls and the audience. In August 2017, it offered a subscription plan of $9.95 per month, less than the price of a movie ticket, to offer its subscribers one movie ticket per day in any cinema hall. The thinking was to establish a large subscriber base and negotiate a bulk pricing discount from cinema hall owners. They also counted on subscribers not using their service very frequently. After all, who would go to the cinema hall to watch a movie every day?

The long-term plan of MoviePass was to become a Netflix of cinema business, including generating its own content. However, not only did the subscribers use the service with great zeal (meaning the company was shelling out more tickets than envisaged), but the negotiations with the cinema halls also did not work out. Thus, even with a monthly subscriber base of 3 million, the service had to be shut down in two years, in September 2019. The cost of running the service was significantly higher than the earnings from the subscriptions.

---

3 See Gartner Forecasts Worldwide Public Cloud Revenue to Grow 17.5 Percent in 2019, consulted in May 2022.

Subscription-based business models rely on a long-term perspective and a lifetime value of their customer base, but the right formulation of a subscription plan is tricky, as it needs to balance fixed costs supported whatever the service reaches a critical mass; and also, variable costs associated with the service – and these can also be dependent on the critical mass to negotiate with suppliers and complementers' specific conditions.

It is therefore in a company's interest to have tiered service plans. That is why Netflix offers basic, standard, and premium service levels with benefits increasing at each level, which lets different family members watch different movies on different screens or in ultra-high-definition resolution if they have a premium subscription. Having different tiers like this generates additional revenue from customers willing to pay more for a more benefit-rich service.

8.3 Monitoring Subscription

In essence, subscription-based business models secure the way revenue is made so that each customer makes recurring payments to access a good or service for a period. Accordingly, it locks in customers to the service and aligns activity KPIs with financial KPIs.

The goal of any subscription plan is to generate enough cash flow from customers' subscription fees to offset outgoing expenses like employee salaries, which it can do effectively. Subscription-based business models rely mainly on five major financial KPIs to "predict" revenue growth – and for which activity KPIs can be aligned to monitor and develop revenue generation.

The Monthly Recurring Revenue (MRR)

This is the main metric (one metric to rule them all!), which defines financially the performance of the business model adopted. It is a clear and sharp way to go beyond the diversity of pricing plans, as it sums up for a defined period (usually monthly) of all the revenue generated.

The calculation is quite simple, as it is the turnover that flows from customers effectively onboarded.

MRR Formula

$$MRR = \sum_{i=1}^{n} (Price.i \times NB.Ci)$$

where Price.i = subscription plan i; and NB.Ci = number of customers for subscription plan i

Imagine a SaaS service with three plans:
- $Plan_1 = 9,99€ - NB.C_1 = 1.000$
- $Plan_2 = 12,99€ - NB.C_2 = 900$
- $Plan_3 = 15,99€ - NB.C_3 = 500$

Then, the MRR is 29.676€.

$$MRR = (9,99 \times 1.000 + 12,99 \times 900 + 15,99 \times 500)$$

Simple as it is, and representing the monthly turnover, the monthly recurring revenue (MRR) needs additional KPIs to decrypt what is at work. So, usually, additional KPIs are used to pilot trends and insights according to growth, customer segments, and the complexity of pricing plans.

- *New MRR*, for example, refers to the MRR generated from new customers onboarded in the defined period (month). It can be interesting to observe whether this number increases or decreases, to reveal pricing plans which perform the best.
- Conversely, *churn MRR* refers to the MRR lost from one period to another due to the unsubscriptions or downgrading in plans. It can reveal a structural problem in the design of the pricing strategy or a cyclical shift in the price elasticity.
- *Add-on MRR* (or expansion MRR) can be relevant if your pricing plan leaves open the possibility of contracting extra features from the initial plan. This KPI can help you reveal which customers are more sensitive to these additional buyings, and the performance of your add-ons.

Like a pilot in the plane, these metrics can help adjust marketing campaigns and reveal the long-term projections, especially the *annual recurring revenue,* by anticipating the balance and annual turnover expected from present customers and periods of subscription.

The Average Revenue per User/Account (ARPU/ARPA)

According to the plans and billing options, the average revenue per user (ARPU) (often used for end-user subscription plans) or average revenue per account (ARPA) (for business subscription plans for multiple users) offer an indication of the average amount to be gained per month / year and per customer.

Calculation and Example of the ARPU/ARPA

$$ARPA = \frac{MRR}{NB.C}$$

where NB.C = Total number of effective customers for a defined period

Reverting to our previous example:
Imagine a SaaS service with three plans:
- Plan1 = 9,99€ – NB.C1 = 1.000
- Plan2 = 12,99€ – NB.C2 = 900
- Plan3 = 15,99€ – NB.C3 = 500

The MRR is 29.676€ and NB.C is 2.400, then

$$ARPA = (29.675 \div 2.400) = 12,365 €$$

Again here, by itself, this metric is quite simple to estimate most customers (those for whom the subscription exceeds the ARPU) contributing to your MRR, and those you should push to shift to an extra plan.

In the same vein, you should look from one month to another at the growth rate for your ARPU/ARPA to monitor whether the growth is in volume or value.

Customer Acquisition Cost

The customer acquisition cost (CAC) (*often called COCA – the cost of customer acquisition*) is not only relevant for subscription-based business models but should be considered as a "killer" metric for all businesses, as it refers to the cost supported in marketing and sales to transform potential leads into effective customers.

Calculation and Example for the CAC

$$CAC = \frac{\text{Total cost of marketing and sales}}{\text{Number of deals closed}}$$

Coming back to our previous example:
Imagine a SaaS service with three plans:
- Plan1 = 9,99€ – NB.C1 = 1.000
- Plan2 = 12,99€ – NB.C2 = 900
- Plan3 = 15,99€ – NB.C3 = 500

During the period, they acquired 300 new customers and budgeted for 15.000€ in marketing and sales in the previous month, then

$$CAC = (15.000 \div 300) = 50 €$$

Each of the 300 customers costs 50€ to acquire. This CAC will be important to track from one period to another to evaluate the performance of acquisition strategies, compared to the ARPA/ARPU generated.

Understanding how much it costs to acquire new customers and identifying the most profitable marketing and sales channels are the key to profitably scaling businesses.
- The CAC will increase with outbound marketing activities such as field sales and paid traffic.
- The CAC will decrease with inbound marketing activities such as word of mouth, organic traffic, viral sales, strategic partnerships, free trials, and affiliation programs.
- The CAC will increase with a low conversion rate, as the business will need more touch to complete a sale.

By encouraging a viral effect through inbound marketing, companies can reduce the CAC to virtually nothing, while opening the door to an ever-larger base of users. For instance, The Dollar Shave Club, a subscription service delivering razors and blades to customers monthly, famously achieved excellent brand awareness and attracted high volumes of new customers through humorous videos that went viral on YouTube. The cost of producing the video was minimal, vis-a-vis the number of views and conversions it generated.

Obviously, a business should recover the CAC in less than 12 months. Otherwise, the business will require too much capital to grow and "subsidise" the acquisition of a customer database.

The Churn Rate

Churn rate refers to the proportion of customers who leave their subscription plan during a given period. It is often an indicator of customer dissatisfaction (intrinsic motivations), cheaper and/or better offers from the competition, aggressive and successful marketing by the competition (extrinsic motivations), or reasons beyond your control, like business failure or strategy shifts.

Calculation and Example for the Churn Rate

$$\text{Churn} = \frac{\text{NB.C}(m-1) - \text{NB.C}(m)}{\text{NB.C}(m-1)}$$

Reverting to our previous example:
   Last month, the company had 2,700 customers [NB.C($m-1$)], and they started the month with 2,560 customers [NB.C(m)]. Then:

$$\text{Churn} = ([2,700 - 2,560] \div 2,700) \simeq 5.2\%$$

Churn can rapidly sink a subscription-based business. Monitoring it from one period to another and understanding what motivates customers to cancel/downgrade their plans is essential to track whether it is due to a bad user experience (low customer satisfaction) or competitiveness of the pricing plan and service. In addition to the raw rate in the volume of customers lost, businesses should consider whether the churn MRR is critical or whether those cancellations impact the majority top tier customers or low-tier customers.

The churn rate will be higher for end-user-oriented businesses but with a smaller impact on MRR, than for business-oriented businesses, for which the impact on MRR will be higher.

Observers assume that a 5–7% annual churn rate is acceptable and related to an organic churn.

Whatever the number, it is important to track the determinants of your cohorts (usage, connections, activity, etc.) to see what can impact your churn positively– i.e., keeping customers active and reducing the probability of a churn. This will impact your cost of customer support.

The Customer Lifetime Value

The final KPI is *customer lifetime value(LTV or sometimes CLV)*. The LTV represents the economic value earned from the customer over the total time they remain a customer.

Thus, LTV is an expectation, which means that it is averaged or statistically inferred.

Calculation and Example for the LTV

$$LTV = \frac{1}{Churn} \times ARPA$$

Coming back to our previous example:
   As Churn $= ([2,700 - 2,560] \div 2,700) \simeq 5.2\%$
   And ARPA $= (29.675 \div 2.400) = 12.365$ €
   Then LTV $= (1 \div 0.052) \simeq 19$ months $\times 12.365 = 237.79$ €

Theoretically, and according to the churn of the period, if activity maintains those KPIs, the company will generate more than 237€ from each customer (a customer remaining a customer for 19 months on average).
   If we compare this number to the CAC, LTV covers 4.75 times the CAC.

The LTV is considered a usual aspect for potential investors to understand the lock-in effect and economic value, which drift from each customer. And as it normally costs less to retain a customer than acquire a new one, this metric is often compared to the CAC.

Observers consider that the LTV should be at least about thrice the CAC for a viable subscription-based business model.

LTV also constitutes a KPI very relevant for assessing the potential of transforming growth into revenue. Thus, it is a key indicator of the sustainability of a business model and exponential profits which investors and founders can expect from scalability – as the cost of service will decrease with the number of users, profits will increase proportionately.

To increase the LTV, a company must continually carry out R&D to improve the quality of service to maintain customers and reduce the churn rate.

8.4 Key Takeaways and Further Considerations

1. Users' appeal for experience rather than ownership makes subscription-based pricing more attractive than one-shot payments.
2. Increasing servitisation relies on the goods/services to be offered through a subscription plan.
3. Due to network effects and resource pooling, subscriptions may be offered at a fraction of the cost of selling the product. The service provider makes money due to the network effect (more subscribers) and resource pooling (lower cost).
4. Recurring billing offers predictable revenue and realigns activity KPIs to financial KPIs.

Why Is Data so Important for SaaS Businesses?

Listening to music informs artists, producers, and music labels about where we listen to music, which songs we like, etc. But, *inter alia*, most importantly, it tells them when we skip songs. This piece of information influences producers in designing the songs. Still, Spotify leverages this to create *ad hoc* playlists that we usually enjoy a lot and that takes away from us even the burden of picking the song we would like to listen to. And this is obviously easier to track than it was with CDs and music tapes.

We can also apply the same reasoning to Netflix: the data collected shapes our experience, suggesting what we see and the likelihood that we will like it.

We can have our smartphone telling us when we should buy something just when we need it or when we should go running and which training session fits our plan the best.

The moment you turn on a digital device, you generate a trail of digital data recognised as your digital footprints. These are linked to:

- **Who you are**, digitally identified with an IP address and a device identification number. And once you are logged into a service, it matches your personal details.
- **Where you are**, as the IP reveals a region; perhaps you activated the access to your location for the service app- then they have a better location of your position.
- **Where you come from**, as the cookies activated behind each Internet page can indicate your buying decision process and reveal patterns of your customer journey
- **When and how long you connect**, as all our connections are time-stamped, and our interactions can be tracked.

These digital footprints can be actively shared by the Internet users and subscribers (by accepting cookies, conditions of use, and conditions of service); or they can be passively generated once the user does not give her/his explicit consent.

Whether they are active or passive digital footprints, they serve a subscription-based business model as its rationales, pushing the firms behind the service to develop resources on data analytics along the customer journey. Data are important in at least three aspects.

First, behind digital subscriptions, we find *data-driven services* and digital products (applications) behind: fuelling the recommendation system to lock customers in the service and continuously improving the user experience on the app. Thus, data are important to objectify and prioritise the product development roadmap so that it can induce partnerships and listing requirements to better match content and users.

Second, a *data-driven company* behind the service can limit and optimise operating costs by revealing the needs and opportunities for the automation of internal processes such as onboarding and customer relationship.

Finally, a *data-driven marketing* effort for which the benefits of data allow better user acquisition and converting processes to customers (funnel of acquisition). Data can help to model the segmentation of customers, predict their actions, and avoid churn (e.g., extend the LTV) with suitable call-to-action to lock them in the subscription.

We just opened a pandora's box of data-driven digital businesses and touched on how important they can be for not only subscriptions but also all digital businesses, as they are born to be "plug and play" with data for better services, at times raising suspicion and ethical concerns. We will revert to that in our concluding chapter.

9 "Free" is Not a Business Model: Business Models Behind Free

Who can boast of not having any free applications on their phone, looking for and testing new web services, especially if they are free, and appreciate being able to do a lot of research on the Internet for free? We are all free riders and digital businesses have understood this. Free access is an integral part of our digital experience, but what are the business models and their characteristics behind this free access? Often used to attract new users rapidly, what are the business challenges behind free-based business models? And can "free" work as a long-term strategy?

9.1 Free as a "Hot Button"

All the top 10 most downloaded apps in the world in 2021 are free to download and free to use. Equally and excluding e-commerce websites, the top 20 most popular websites in the world are also accessible at least partly for free. These illustrate the prominence of 'free' in the digital economy. Most digital users consult their emails, connect with friends, read the news, watch videos, and listen to music for free. And yet, there is another ranking that is worth considering. The ranking of the apps is according to the level of revenue they generate. Here, the app that tops the list is also free to download and partially free to use. This app–the dating app Tinder–offers free and premium subscriptions. This is called a "freemium" model: consumers can download the app and get access to a certain range of features for free, but if they want to use the app's full range of features, they need to pay. These rankings illustrate the counter-intuitive and paradoxical nature of 'free' as a business model. It can be seen as a marketing tool to achieve scale but can also be the foundation of a powerful business model. In this section, we review the marketing function of 'free' and then turn our attention to the diverse types of free-based business models.

The popular adage *There is no such thing as a free lunch* conveys the idea that it is impossible to get something for nothing. The "free lunch" in the saying refers to the formerly common practice in American bars of offering a "free lunch" to entice drinking customers. So, "free" is very rarely free. In this case, users will pay for something else – for example, the drink. If a group of users does not pay for anything, then they probably have their own intrinsic value. For example, nightclubs may offer free entrance to women. Women who tend to drink less may not be the ultimate target. Instead, through such a promotion, clubs expect to attract the more profitable "men segment". However, men want to meet women; hence the need to offer women a free pass. In other words, men will pay for admission and drinks to meet women. "Meeting women" constitutes an element of the value proposition offered to men by the nightclub. It is the real "job-to-be-done", for which the value proposition of the nightclub captures the value.

Digital companies use similar tricks. For instance, when users access Google's search engine for free, they essentially become part of the value proposition to attract paying advertisers. Many digital companies provide a free basic offer. The dating app Tinder lets users "swipe to date" but gives them only a limited number of opportunities to do so. If users want unlimited swipes, they must pay a monthly subscription fee for the premium service. Likewise, Dropbox offers a small amount of free cloud storage in the hope that users upgrade to its premium plans. Finally, Netflix offers a free month of their service to new users hoping that they would continue after this expires. By asking customers to enter their credit card details before receiving their free month, they still can be automatically billed, should they forget to cancel before the trial ends.

9.2 Who/What Subsidises the Value?

The previous examples range from short-term marketing tactics to potentially long-term sustainable marketing strategies. They illustrate the idea that "free is not really for free". Users will pay later or for something else; otherwise, someone else will pay instead of them or literally for them. Google, Tinder, Dropbox, and Netflix do not have the same digital business model. Instead, 'free' is used differently from one business model to the other.

A Constellation of Free-Based Business Models

Because there is no associated value capture with the "free" offers, there is no business model if the company's plan does not go further than the free offer. Business models, defined as a company's plan for making a profit, imply revenue models. Hence, 'free' can be a business model only if a subsidy process is involved. This subsidy may be provided by a diverse set of stakeholders and can serve different strategies behind free-based business models. Based on the seminal work of Anderson (2009) in the book *Free: The Future of a Radical Price*, four distinct subsidy mechanisms can be identified (Figure 9-A). The subsidy technique enables companies to still capture value while operating a "free-based" business model.

Cross subsidy: In this configuration, a product is offered for free with the expectation of making money from another related product (often requiring repeated purchases of consumables). This technique can also be called "razor and blades" or "hook and bait". The basic product (bait/razor) is offered cheaply or for free; the complementary product or refill (hook/blades) is sold expensively. The basic product cannot be used without the complementary product. A similar mechanism exists in the

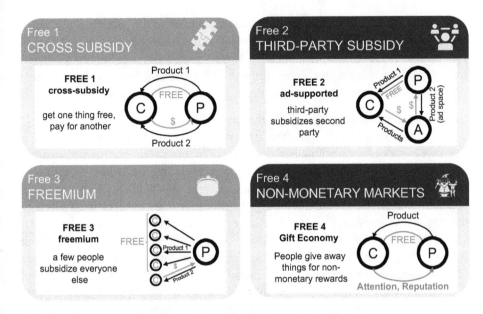

Figure 9-A: Subsidy Mechanisms Behind Free-Based Business Models.
(Adapted from Anderson, 2009)

traditional economy. Printer companies sell printers at a low price and make money on cartridge purchases; even Nespresso machines are available for an affordable compensation of 1 euro in exchange for the subscription to monthly billing of credits for Nespresso Pods.

Some apps use this strategy to entice and connect with users and sell in-app tools to extend the user experience. The most downloaded mobile app video games include "Clash of Clans", "Angry Birds", "Candy Crush", "Hill Climb Racing", and "Subway Surfers". They are all free but all of them also practise in-app purchases. The average spending of Clash of Clans users, for example, is $112. In-app purchases may include full game unlock, bonus game levels, game currency, such as coins or gems, or simply removing painful ads.

Third-party subsidy: This category epitomises the adage "if it's free, you are the product". The product or service is free for the end-users, subsidised by a third party. In many cases, the third party is a business side, often advertisers who wish to reach a targeted user base. Google's search engine and Facebook (Meta) are such examples where third-party advertisers pay the company to access users. Advertisers pay the platform when users click on their advertisements and watch their promotional videos so that ultimately, they visit their website and buy their services. We (as users) passively accept and appreciate this mechanism: how many times do we go on page 2 of results on Google?

Freemium: In this scenario, a basic service is provided to the users free of charge. The service is subsidised by a small number of users (*people subsidy*)–as few as 1% – who subscribe to the premium offer. Music streaming service Spotify, for example, offers a free version and a premium one with additional features. The next section discusses the freemium model in detail.

Non-monetary markets (the gift economy): The company provides a free product/service/content *in exchange for attention or brand reputation*. Google offered a free Wi-Fi service to the millions of users of the Indian railway, as part of a corporate social responsibility initiative but also to promote Internet usage – which ultimately led to the usage of their product and services. Wikipedia is another example of a non-monetary market. Here, experts contribute articles on specialist subjects to the site, which acts as a platform they can use to build their reputation. *The Guardian* newspaper in the UK also proposes to its readers to "support our journalism with a contribution of any size". The same is the case with influencers on YouTube or other social platforms who create tutorials, reviews, and so on, in the hope of gaining followers. Ultimately, these influencers can develop a third-party subsidy business model. This happens when brands provide free products or pay social media influencers to mention them in sponsored blogs or posts to reach the influencers' followers.

Offering something free in the short run may appear unsustainable. However, as we will discuss now, it can also lay the economic foundation to develop a scalable digital business model.

The Underlying Rationale for a "Free" Strategy

As seen earlier, a traditional business model implies a value exchange. Companies provide something of value to consumers, who in return offer money. "Free" is, therefore, a very risky strategy/tactic, as businesses need to develop an offering without receiving the normal necessary monetary exchange for the value they have created. Hence, before initiating such strategies, it is necessary to review the conditions under which they make sense. Those conditions depend on the characteristics of the offering or the market.

Offering's Rationale for Free

'Free' is the proverbial carrot dangled before the users to give them the sense that they have "nothing-to-lose" in the absence of a monetary recompense, besides the time spent and data provided as investments. For the entrepreneurs, this free experience good/service should remain financially sustainable.

The financial attributes of the service/product are important to consider. Free offerings are easier to deploy when they do not imply variable costs or only marginal ones for the cost per unit. It is not surprising in this sense to see several players across different industries adopting a free offering in their business model: software as a service (SaaS) (Dropbox, Slack), media portals (Facebook, Newsfeeds websites, YouTube), bit vendors (App Editors), search agents (TripAdvisor), and so on. Accordingly, instead of developing new features, entrepreneurs can present their minimum feature set to a large audience for free, as a way for experiencing their basic services and gaining traction in their markets.

In the world of digital business and network economies, the law of marginal cost is an important economic motivator. When deploying its network, a business must cover its start-up costs while investing in supporting infrastructure. However, once the infrastructure is in place, the cost of each new user is close to zero – what we call the law of marginal costs adapted to network economies: *If the cost to serve a customer (support aside) is close to zero, the long-term price of the product in the market will be zero (because of competitive pressure).*[1] That remains the case until a point is reached where no more users can be accommodated without adversely affecting the service and the cost to serve.

Their enormous capacity is the reason mobile phone service providers can incrementally increase the amount of data offered with their monthly plans. Just a few years ago, an average plan might have offered 5 GB of data. Now, 20 or 40 GB data plans are standard, with some plans even offering unlimited data. Most customers signup for the large data plan because they want the comfort of knowing they can use their phones without running the risk of incurring unexpected charges. However, if they were to check, they might find that they are using only 10 GB of data per month on average – that is, nowhere near their data limit. Hence, offering 40 GB per month is a useful marketing strategy for mobile phone carriers, as it costs them nothing. Even if a few users come close to or even exceed their data plan limit, the carrier has the capacity to accommodate them at virtually no cost.

For start-ups, this means the flow of marginal costs is reversed, as they know the long-term cost will be zero. As Anderson put it: "when something halves in price each year, zero is inevitable" (Anderson, 2010, 163). By starting with a cost of zero to the customer, they can lock in long-term users in the hope they will subscribe to a paid-for plan, or the advertisers will flock to the platform seeking access to a wide user base. Accordingly, they anticipate the lifetime value of their customers at the price of negative cash flow in the short run. Thus, free is not essentially free of financial consequences for digital ventures. It needs to be subsidised by other stakeholders (shareholders by raising money in this case).

---

1 The Complete Guide to Freemium Business Models, blog article on TechCrunch (September 5, 2011) – accessed on April 14, 2022.

9.3 Mind the Paywall

The Critical Mass Imperative

Digital ventures sometimes bring radically new value propositions, implying that the user experience does not compare to any known customer journey. In those cases, companies need to find ways to give a taste of the new experience and entice initial users.

In this context, *free is undoubtedly a huge accelerator of the adoption of novelty*. On streaming platforms' highly competitive battlefield, "free" is a way to lock in the user. It allows to quickly reach a critical mass of users to validate the minimum viable product, convince investors to back up the scaling phase, and reach a dominant position before the competitors.

Whatever the configuration, somewhere and/or at some time, someone must pay to ensure the sustainability of the business. The risk is that free users become reluctant to become long-term paying customers. *When people get used to "not paying" for a service, it becomes more difficult to get even a penny from them.* This is called the "penny gap". This expression means that there is a market for a "free" offering and no market at all for a paid solution, no matter how cheap it is.

Playing on the emotional hot button of "free" has radically changed since the beginning of the Internet. People are now used to free and expect free digital offerings. Mobile phone users download dozens of free apps and are equally used to free social media platforms. Those behaviours may also affect SaaS providers or streaming platforms. Further, many consumers have developed a "multi-homing strategy" for their cloud storage by creating profiles on different cloud storage services before reaching the size limit of the free service.

Free can rapidly become a market entry necessity. If this is the case, then companies have to offer a free taste of the service at least for a limited period and/or limited features. But *companies need to pay attention to their customers, not only users*. In that sense, companies do not have to engage specific financial resources to attract "free users". This psychological price should be by itself a marketing tactic to attract users, *a viral lift*. The more users are satisfied with the service, the more they become ambassadors and promoters to their connections: *spreading the word of mouth* at no marketing costs for the company to attract new users. If the viral lift works perfectly, the marketing activities will be focused on the conversion of free users into customers and the lock-in of users by enhancing features and encouraging them to connect often to the service.

Then, Is "Free" Part of a Long-term Strategy or a Short-term Tactic?

The answer depends on the company's vision and how they integrate the scaling ambition into this vision. Reid Hoffman, the founder of LinkedIn, named this strategy Blitzscaling in a reference to the blitzkrieg performed by the German Army during

World War II: *Blitzscaling is what you do when you need to grow really, really quickly. It's the science and art of rapidly building out a company to serve a large and usually global market, with the goal of becoming the first mover at scale. [. . .] If a start-up determines that it needs to move very fast, it will take on far more risk than a company going through the normal, rational process of scaling up.* (Interview with Reid Hoffman in Harvard Business Review, May 2016, 46)

Accordingly, "free" can be seen as a short-term tactic to grow quickly and scale faster than competitors, even if it implies cumulative losses to subsidise the adoption curve and learn during this period on which customer segments to focus on, to quickly balance the cumulative losses during ignition and scale phases and starting to compensate costs by a worldwide base revenue stream.

As we will see now, with freemium, the question of keeping the offer free in the long run remains open, as the novelty of the service wears off and the penny gap makes it difficult to convert users into customers.

Free + Premium = Freemium

As described previously, intuitively, when we figure out some free-based business models, we refer easily to freemium, where a few customers subsidise a large base of free riders. Let us introduce some key characteristics and challenges faced by businesses in this context.

The key idea behind freemium can be summarised thus:

> Give your service away for free, possibly ad supported but maybe not, acquire a lot of ~~customers~~ [users] very efficiently through word-of-mouth, referral networks, organic search marketing, etc., then offer premium priced value-added services or an enhanced version of your service to your customer base. (Quoted from Fred Wilson on his blog, in March 2006)

This is how Fred Wilson, a personality in the US landscape of venture capitalists, described a common pattern of business plans he received at the time. As he was asking in his blog post for a name for this business model, one of his followers suggested "freemium".

Beyond the catchy story of wording concepts with the crowd, we have here the foundations of a generic pattern to create, deliver, and capture value – viz., a business model.

In a "freemium" business model, a product or service is offered free alongside a premium subscription version. The free version is the hot button that encourages users to try the service in the hope that they will adopt it and some of them will pay for it and subsidise the free riders. If the "people subsidy" mechanism is a systemic understanding of this archetype business model, Fred Wilson also sought a way to describe how these businesses, particularly the cash-strapped ones, were using innovative and viral marketing strategies and tactics like word-of-mouth, referrals, and organic search to cut the cost of gaining traction and acquiring new users – which became known as *growth hacking*.

Freemium: Blitzscaling or Long-term Strategy?

Strategists at companies using freemium business models must really understand their markets if they are to attract sufficient new users through outbound marketing activities, as well as enhance and promote service quality to premium customers so they continue to subscribe. By employing growth hacking tactics to attract free users, more of the marketing budget can be aimed at premium customers. By treating them well, the business can increase the potential for referrals and cut its churn rate by converting more free users to premium plans.

Besides using freemium as a short-term marketing tactic to capture many individual users, some businesses use it as a long-term strategy to penetrate business markets. Dropbox encourages the uptake of its service by rewarding everyone with free storage. It employs free offers to full advantage by creating a viral lift through three service tiers – a free Dropbox Basic, Dropbox Pro, and Dropbox Business. Since those who want to share and receive files through Dropbox must both have accounts, the service makes it extremely easy to invite others on board. In fact, it incentivises them to do so. For example, if a university lecturer uses Dropbox to share files with students, they get additional storage for "recruiting" them, as will those students when they, in turn, recruit new Dropbox users. The higher number of new users someone recruits, the more free storage they receive. Dropbox does this in the hope that when these students graduate and some of them start their own companies, they will convert to the subscription service because they see the benefits of using Dropbox in business. Thus, the real revenue for Dropbox comes from B2B subscription plans based on user numbers, storage amounts and other services.

In freemium business models, revenue can also be generated by monetising the data gathered by the service. If data can be valued for a third-party stakeholder, then gathering data can be a long-term strategy, as it enables better profiling. This means ads and information can be more effectively targeted at users based on the way they use the service, such as the type of music they listen to.

The app economy has also reinvented freemium business models through in-app payments. While the TV show South Park may have satirised free gaming apps as *just barely fun*, many have proven addictive, hooking players by offering a limited number of free games but then requiring in-app payment to keep playing or advance to the next level. The payments, though small, sometimes less than a dollar or Euro, add up when millions of users make them. Some paid applications also offer in-app purchases. A photo-editing application, for instance, might include a limited range of filters as part of the original purchase, with the option to buy additional filters later. Invesp reports that as of 2017, while just over 5% of the users spent money on in-app purchases, global sales from the in-app purchases were pegged at $37 billion.

Candy Crush Saga is a mobile gaming app that lets users make in-app purchases to acquire "extra lives" or access additional features. Its growth strategy revolves around creating a game that is sufficiently addictive to go viral. In 2013, it did just that, with over 300 million playing the game by the end of the fourth quarter. Of these, 12.2 million made in-app purchases, a conversion rate of 4%. It is estimated that the app earned around $693 million in 2018 through in-app purchases across Google Play and the App Store.

Candy Crush Saga illustrates just how a free offer can act as a hot button that attracts users. If a company's ambition is to go global and its service costs the same whether it has 10 million or 300 million users, even a relatively small percentage of paying users is enough to create a lucrative business when the service goes viral.

Though less visible than premium subscription offers, *in-app payments are the new freemium*, relying on the "barely fun" aspect of games to create an addictive quality that expands the user database through the social value derived from word-of-mouth recommendations and user referrals. Conversions to paid use are encouraged through micropayments that are so small they seem inconsequential, but which may add up to more than the cost of a subscription plan. Such micropayments are also a source of controversy, with children clicking payment buttons to continue playing a game on their parents' phones or tablets, without realising they are accumulating charges on mum or dad's credit cards.

When determining whether to adopt a freemium business model, a company must consider three questions:

1. *How big does the company want to become?* If the goal is to create a dominant worldwide platform within a specific industry, a free offer should be a short-term tactic and possibly even a long-term strategy.
2. *What will be the value of free users?* Will the free offer be a downgraded version of the premium offer, or will it include only basic features? In other words, when explaining the value of being a free user, the company also must explain the value of being a premium customer.
3. *How much will it cost to serve free users?* Before embarking on a freemium strategy, a company must be sure the cost of free users is close to zero and that they can count on a viral lift from word-of-mouth, referrals, and incentives to rapidly reach a critical mass of users. Once this is achieved, marketing activities should be focused on converting free users into premium ones, while retaining those already acquired. This aspect is detailed in the last section.

The key to determining whether a business model is truly freemium is revenue generation. *If most of the revenue stream does not come from the premium offer, then the company is not a freemium company.*

For instance, though LinkedIn began with a freemium business model, its premium offer no longer generates most of its revenue. By 2018, premium subscriptions represented just a small portion (17%) of LinkedIn's revenue, the majority of which was from its talent solution (65%) and marketing solutions (18%). In the long run, instead of premium account payments, data generated by free users have proven valuable for LinkedIn, as this can be used for marketing and to generate brand awareness. User profile data is also valuable to recruitment companies and HR departments wanting to identify suitable job candidates. Thus, it has not remained a freemium company, as the real value proposition now no longer revolves around individuals but businesses, making revenue generation B2B-oriented.

Key Performance Indicators behind "People Subsidy" Mechanisms

As a starting point, *critical mass* refers to the minimum number of users required to get the business model operational. *Critical mass should not be confused with the breakeven point*, which relates to the number of customers required to balance service costs. For an online game, the critical mass would be the number of players needed at any given time. For a communication tool, *the critical mass refers to the minimum number of users required to spark the initial liquidity to find value in the service.* This metric is not associated specifically with the freemium business model, as it is mostly dependent and required for any network-based service – for example, a service for which the value is dependent on the participation of at least two sides. But in the context of freemium, the critical mass will depend on the viral lift which can enhance the outbound marketing and limit inbound marketing to develop and sustain the initial adoption of free users.

As mentioned previously, the freemium business model involves a "people subsidy", as premium users' payments support the free users of the service.

> The easiest way to get 1 million people paying is to get 1 billion people using (Phil Libin, Founder of Evernote)

In a freemium business, the critical mass must be known to calculate the percentage of users the business must attempt to convert to premium users. To be sustainable, freemium relies on the big numbers required to support a consistent revenue stream. So, one of the key performance indicators (KPIs) for the freemium business model is the *conversion rate*, which refers to the percentage of users who decide to adopt the premium version of the service. By monitoring this metric, a business can gauge how successful they are at bridging the penny gap. By experience, this ratio is often low: 4% conversion rate for Dropbox, 0.5% for Google Drive, and 4.1% for

Evernote. In other words, out of every 100 users, there are just 2 to 4 who become paying customers. When Phil Libin mentions a far lower conversion rate (1/1,000 instead of 1/100), it is a prudential way to design the costs of the service and not overestimate the adoption rate necessary to support an expected conversion rate. Because a freemium business model requires such large numbers of users, it is of the greatest applicability to companies with ambitions to reach millions, if not billions, of users, and function as global services and companies.

Before being acquired by Facebook (Meta), messaging app WhatsApp employed an interesting revenue generation strategy by making the first year of usage free but charging an annual fee of $0.99 thereafter. This gave users time to establish chat groups on the app and to experience the convenience of communicating with friends anywhere in the world at a low cost. After enjoying these benefits, users were more than happy to pay the virtually insignificant follow-on fee. This locked them in and overcame the penny gap. Considering that the platform had 500 million users and was growing at a rate of 1 million users per day, even such a small annual fee had the potential to generate over $500 million in annual revenue. This, of course, changed once the application was acquired by Facebook which decided to subsidise the service and maintain it free for its users after the year test.

Then comes an important metric for the sustainability of the freemium model: the *freemium ratio*, which is the number of premium users required to subsidise free users. For instance, a ratio of 1/10 would mean that one premium user is needed to support nine free users.

To Have a Sustainable Freemium Business Model, the Conversion Rate Should be Greater than the Freemium Ratio.

Let us understand these ratios using some examples (see box below). For simplicity of calculation, assume that each user costs the business €1 to serve and a single premium user is charged €10 – that is, covers 10 users (including him(her)self). A freemium ratio of 10% means that out of every 100 users, 10 would convert to premium. Thus, there would be no profit or loss. If the conversion rate is 1/5, 2 out of every 10 users would convert to premium and the business is profitable with a €5 margin for each premium user. If the conversion rate is below 1/10, say 1/15 – less than the freemium ratio – the business loses money, and the freemium business model would not be sustainable.

A Simulation of Freemium KPIs
Conversion rate of 1/10 (10 free users are required to get a premium user)
Cost of acquisition and service: €1*10 = €10 (*cost structure*)
Premium VP: €10*1 = €10 (*revenue stream*)
Margin = €0 (*break-even*)
Conversion rate of 1/5 (five free users are required to get a premium user)
Cost of acquisition and service: €1*5 = €5 (*cost structure*)
Premium VP: €10*1 = €10 (revenue stream)
Margin = €5 (*profit*)
Conversion rate of 1/15 (15 free users are required to get a premium user)
Cost of acquisition and service: €1*15 = €15 (*cost structure*)
Premium VP: €10*1 = €10 (*revenue stream*)
Margin = €5 (loss)

Similarly, to any subscription-based business model (as we will explore in the next chapter), the sustainability of a freemium business model depends on paying customer loyalty. This can be described by two KPIs:

The *customer lifetime value* (CLV) refers to the revenue stream generated by a customer as long as he/she remains a customer of the service. Understanding the lifetime value of diverse types of premium users can help determine how best to direct marketing activities. For instance, LinkedIn Premium marketing would be better off targeting salespeople searching for leads as well as professional users, who are likely to have a greater CLV, than targeting a job seeker. According to your subscription plan structure for the premium service, CLV is dependent on the pricing plan adopted and the duration a customer remains a customer.

The duration will be impacted by the *churn rate*, which is the proportion of customers or subscribers who leave the service during a given period (yearly or monthly). The reasons can vary from low quality of service or a better service offered by a competitor.

Evernote was another successful freemium business model. This famous app for note taking, organising, and task management was very efficient in the design of their service and the monitoring of KPIs to be sustainable. In a founder's interview in 2010, Phil Libin shared their books and emphasised the key elements to pave the freemium performance:

Two conditions of value proposition design are:
1. *The way the product/service is designed* should influence a significant portion of free users to cross the paywall.
2. *The more a user spends time on the service*, the more he/she values it, and the more this user is closer to hitting the free service limit.

And three steps to pave the freemium success:
1. *Win millions of free users*: Freemium sustainability is primarily dependent on a large adoption base, which should be acquired at a low cost (no customer acquisition cost for the free users) by extensive outbound marketing strategies and a viral lift.
2. *Convert more active users to premium status over time*: The path of conversion should improve over time to demonstrate the sustainability of the freemium model and also on an organic basis, as the free riders spend time on the service.
3. *Keep costs down,* whether they are associated with customer acquisition or the cost of the service. Again, those costs should be mainly fixed not to be dependent on the volume of service and explode with the number of users and customers on board.

In 2013, Evernote was considered a unicorn – a start-up with a valuation above 1 billion dollars:
–   41 million users were active in 2013 versus 34 million in 2010.
–   1.5 million premium users in 2013 (3.7% conversion rate) versus 1.4 million in 2010 (4.1% as conversion rate in 2010).
–   Gross revenue was estimated at $0.25 per premium customer ($0.09 towards costs and $0.16 as net profit).
–   These metrics supported an expanding product range over time to sustain continuous growth.

9.4 Key Takeaways and Further Considerations

1. To be a business model, 'free' needs a revenue mechanism. Free-based business models rely on subsidy mechanisms, whether they are features, people, third parties, or a non-monetary counterpart of free riders.
2. The Freemium model works by offering basic services free and premium/business services for a payment.
3. The freemium strategy works only with many users.
4. In the absence of other revenue sources, freemium may not be a sustainable business model in the long run.

A Value Proposition Canvas for Freemium?

As noted earlier, in the freemium model, the free offers are used to introduce a new service or product that consumers could use at no cost. The free service is used as a hot button to entice would-be buyers to try out the novelty aspect of a value proposition. Freemium business models require a value proposition canvas (Figure 9-B) different from the traditional business model or that of the two-sided platform because, with freemium, the canvas must present separate value propositions for free and premium customers.

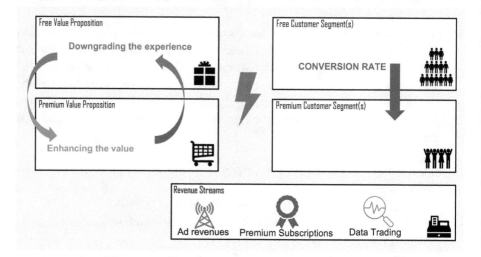

Figure 9-B: Proposition of an Adapted Value Proposition Canvas for Freemium.

Moreover, the business must also define a limit, or paywall, at which value is either enhanced for premium customers or downgraded for free users. There is a difference between the two approaches. In some business models, the premium offer extends the number of features available to users. LinkedIn Premium is an example. Here, premium users get access to InMail and can see who has viewed their profile. In contrast, Spotify keeps the value of its free offer low by exposing free users to ads. This is done in the hope that the users would jump to the premium plan to avoid being annoyed by promotional messages when listening to music.

10 Looking Forward: Is Winter Coming?

Our approach was to present some broad features that were so specific and/or representative of digital business configuration that they deserved to be treated as a business model in a dedicated chapter. Our approach revealed some common threads. In this conclusion, we focus on those common patterns revolving around the notion of customer intimacy and data. Data have been one of the common threads throughout this book. We then reflect on the domination and concentration of players in digital markets. Finally, we analyse emerging current patterns of the digital economy and eco-system to consider whether a dark "winter is coming" or whether a brighter "future is already there"?

Our analysis of business models has presented some categories of methods of creating and capturing value. This was not a precise taxonomy of mutually exclusive and collectively exhaustive shapes of possible business models. Companies can have a social platform element combined with a subsidised ad (free) or freemium value capture mechanism based on subscription business models. This very much describes LinkedIn, for example. In this concluding chapter, we analyse the common thread of data and its implications, before looking at the future of digital businesses.

10.1 Customer Intimacy, Data, and Its Implications

We live in a world abounding with data. The ubiquity of digital and mobile technology implies that most of our movements, interactions with apps, websites, and friends generate data. Whatever we do, we leave digital footprints behind every action. This presents both huge opportunities and challenges for digital companies.

Customer Intimacy and Data-Driven Opportunities

The most successful and omnipotent digital players in each of the business categories described earlier (sharing economy, marketplace, software as a service, social platform, etc.) share a level of understanding and a proximity with users that is virtually unmatched. This understanding is sometimes–but rarely–based on a fantastic intuition. Steve Jobs is often cited as an example of someone who had a vision that no market data could have instigated (e.g., the iPad). Yet, for all the related services of Apple, as well as most of the services offered by Google, Facebook, Microsoft, Hubspot, Amazon, and BlaBlaCar, user data is key in predicting and shaping the next wave of offerings.

In the B2C markets, these companies have all developed an app, which, if used regularly, literally means that they have penetrated the intimacy of users. Several studies have proposed that the mobile phone is an extension of the human self.[1] Most of us are incapable of separating ourselves from our phone and when we do, most likely by accident, we feel incomplete. That is because smartphones contain information that used to be stored in our brain (now retrieved on the Internet via Google), social connections that used to be made physically (Facebook, Instagram), mood that used to be dictated by our hearts (now triggered by a playlist on Spotify). It is the thumb that allowed us to hitchhike (now replaced by the BlaBlaCar App), the arm that hailed a taxi (Uber), the feet that walked us to the store (Amazon), the cinema (Netflix), the bookies (Bet365, PaddyPower), and so on. This consumer intimacy produces data about who, when, where, what, how, with whom, and how often, in combination with what other things users watch, scroll, listen, hear, exchange, sell, and, most importantly, buy. In 2020, IBM estimated that every person generated 1.7 megabytes of data per second! Intimacy belongs to users, but data belong to the app owner. Digital businesses are in a unique position to exploit this.

We already saw how data were instrumental to the success of Netflix. Using advanced data and analytics, Netflix can provide users with personalised movie and TV show recommendations, as well as marketing trailers, predict the popularity of original content, and therefore optimise production planning, and as any other business, inform and enhance decision-making. According to some commentators, Netflix saves $1 billion per year on customer retention because of data exploitation. Similar reasoning – possibly with less impressive figures – could be applied to most of the companies that have been mentioned in this book. Data are the new oil. Exploiting Data is and will continue to be at the heart of digital business models, whether it is to continuously improve the service and the business or even capture value from it through a data trading business model.

Data trading, the Example of Twitter

Twitter is one of the pioneers in this field of data exploitation. In 2012, the American social network created the Twitter Political Index, a live tool that was measuring the sentiment of the tweets related to Barack Obama and Mitt Romney during the presidential campaign. At the time, it was an innovative experiment to show the value embedded in the tweets. Soon, Twitter transformed this experiment into a real service. At first, it licensed all tweets to a selected pool of companies that could sell data to universities, market research agencies, and so on.

Tweets are an incredible source of value. They are public (the goal of Twitter is to share your thoughts with anyone interested in the topic, through the hashtags, and not only with your friends or followers), and can give great insights on what a (significant) part of the world thinks on a given topic in real time.

Therefore, Twitter stops making all the tweets directly available through the internal search engine, while organisations can buy access to the tweet stream on a given topic for research purposes. After some years, Twitter made this business line internal and declared data licensing among its revenue sources.

---

1 Belk, R. W. (2013). Extended Self in a Digital World. Journal of Consumer Research, 40(3), 477–500.

This model is called "data trading"; Twitter is probably one of the earliest cases, and one of the most virtuous. Still, it is not the only one (Trabucchi et al., 2017). The value embedded in data is simply too relevant to be overlooked*.

*See other examples and further developments on that in Trabucchi, D., Buganza, T., & Pellizzoni, E. (2017). Give Away Your Digital Services: Leveraging Big Data to Capture Value. Research-Technology Management, 60(2), 43–52.

Yet, it is precisely this grey area between the privacy and intimacy of users overlapping the ownership and exploitation of data by businesses that creates tensions and crises. So far, data-driven businesses have been able to trade on the online behaviour of users, which does not seem to match their privacy concerns.

Data (Privacy) Concerns and Regulatory Considerations

Human beings are complex. Users of digital services have expressed concerns over the use of their personal data. A 2021 KPMG report titled "Corporate Data Responsibility: Bridging the Trust Chasm" reports that 86% of the Internet users feel a growing concern about data privacy, while 78% expressed fears about the amount of data being collected. They seem ill-informed about the specifics of the data collected, by whom and for what purpose. Despite this, they remain reluctant to change their online privacy behaviour or limit their online activity. Rather than showing restraint in online data sharing behaviour, users seem to be voluntarily posting extremely personal information about themselves online for the world to see.

This apparent contradiction between online privacy concerns and actual online privacy behaviour is called the privacy paradox. There are several factors that could explain this contradiction, including a lack of knowledge. Few people read privacy policies, while others find the information too difficult to comprehend. Poor interface design, and in some cases, interface complexity, certainly contribute to this problem. Facebook, for example, has approximately 50 settings and more than 170 options, just for privacy alone; therefore, it is little surprise that users have severe problems with handling privacy settings on SNSs.

In any case, regulators have eventually taken into consideration the concerns of the public. The 2018 implementation of the General Data Protection Regulation (GDPR) in the European Union represents an effort by regulators to push back against increasingly data-reliant digital business models. The GDPR attempts to protect user privacy, requiring firms to notify users about how their data will be used, so that they may provide informed consent. GDPR "obliges the controller to take appropriate technical and organisational measures to implement data protection principles to ensure that by default only personal data that are necessary for each specific purpose of the processing are processed". The United States is following suit, in terms of privacy regulation, with California passing the California Privacy Protection Act,[2] which is similar to the GDPR. One could argue that the new regulations regarding privacy data are coming a little late and may have a relatively limited impact, while the GDPR, for example, does not constrain the errant behaviour of digital businesses. Users do not necessarily have a choice; they are simply made aware that their data is being used but cannot refuse the terms and conditions of the service. Corporate interests typically eschew regulation, and industry self-regulation has shown its limits for protecting user privacy on numerous occasions. There is a case for introducing regulations before a pattern of data usage emerges. It seems incredibly difficult for regulators to introduce effective regulations once an entire data privacy industry and business ecosystem has been established. Regulations were introduced in 2018, 10 to 20 years after Google, Facebook, YouTube, etc. became mainstream media.

Most corporate technological giants are struggling with the challenge of balancing a data monetisation business model with protecting the privacy of their users. Apple, Amazon, Netflix, Spotify, and YouTube have all recently been hit with accusations of GDPR breaches by allegedly failing to provide basic information to citizen requests, such as how they buy, share, and store user data, a violation of the "right to access" enshrined in Article 15 of the GDPR.

It is difficult to envisage a future with less data. Data embed so much value that it would simply be a waste not to leverage them to create value for companies, users, and society. Nevertheless, the current situation seems hardly sustainable. Perhaps the order of priority for creating value should be reversed: society first, then users, and then companies. Users who are also citizens are continuing to raise important and valid questions such as: Is privacy now considered a matter of democracy? Should our personal data be a tradable good?

Data may be the real oil of the years to come. Digital businesses should therefore be aware of the hazardous nature of oil, if they want to avoid disasters such as the Deepwater Horizon oil spill.

10.2 Winners of Today and Winter of Tomorrow

The Red Queen effect refers to the increased pressure to adapt faster just to survive. It is driven by an increase in the evolutionary pace of rival technology solutions (Barnett & Hansen, 1996). Many businesses already feel that it takes all the running you can just to keep in the same place. No matter what they do, they will never catch up with the digital giants.

---

2 See Government of the State of California. (2013). Privacy Laws. (Accessed: 26 May 2022).

Winners-Take-All Dynamics

Tech Giants, "Big Five", previously named as GAMAM, represent the big winners from the decades of digital adoption, technology, and business developments underlying them.

In 2021, Alphabet, Amazon, Apple, Meta, and Microsoft represented on their own more than $1,4 trillion in revenue – equal, for example, to the Brazilian GDP, as pointed out by Visual Capitalist[3] analysing their 10-k reports. It continues to trust the top tier of most value companies in the world.

Amazon is the most impressive, with total revenue close to $470 billion in 2021 – largely supported by the original eCommerce activity but sustained in net income by clouding services.

Apple generates the highest net income in volume with almost $95 billion for a $366 billion revenue in 2021 – more than 80% of which is from hardware sales (iPhone, iPad, Mac, and wearables), whereas services generate the highest gross margins.

Alphabet dominates the online advertising industry, which sustains its revenues and net income. More than 85% of all Internet searches are done on Google search engines, and thanks to this large and massive user base, Alphabet generates a strong 30% net profit margin and $76 billion in net income.

Microsoft has the most diversified revenue sources with clouding services, subscriptions to Office products, and royalties on the Windows operating system. Microsoft has the highest 36% net profit margin and is more focused on B2B than B2C.

Meta is still the largest social media platform, with approximately 2.9 billion monthly active users. If they generate the lowest revenues and net income among the Big Five (close to $118 billion in revenue and $40 billion in net income), Meta generated for 2021 an impressive average revenue per user higher than $40.

These numbers are stunning confirmation, if at all needed, of winner-takes-all benefits and dynamics, as these Big Five were able to capture a disproportionately large share of the value in their own industries. This was possible due to the strong network effects at work in their market configurations, the strong brand effects they created, the high multi-homing costs (especially on social networks) and the extensive use of big data and machine learning to continue to lock-in users and sides on board.

All these Big Five reached a position of dominance worldwide and game changing in advertising, media, commerce, applications, etc. Even if they were not initially directly fighting in the same industries, they constituted giant ecosystems and digital conglomerates operating and fixing the rules of the game in the digital arena. They have strong brands, financial power, and trust technology developments. Even

---

3 "How Do Big Tech Giants Make Their Billions?", Published on Visualcapitalist on April 25, 2022 – and consulted in May 2022.

if governments–especially in the US and EU–are gradually enforcing anti-trust legislations, they are here to stay and shape our present and future realities; as they opened it in the past, why does it matter now?

The Red Tape of Self-Organised Creative Destruction?

From the traditional players' viewpoint, the Big Five have been perceived as disruptors and game changers in their initial industries. Digital was catalyst for value creation, as it opened up new avenues to exploit the technologies and reshape business model potentialities.

Disruption is a word often associated with digital business. Coined by the economist Clayton Christensen in the 1990s, disruption refers to *A process by which a product or service takes root initially in simple applications at the bottom of a market – typically by being less expensive and more accessible–and then relentlessly moves up-market, eventually established displacing competitors* (Christensen Institute[4]).

At the core of all digital disruption dynamics, we find the Schumpeter's gale and the famous work of the economist Joseph Schumpeter on "creative destruction" which he defines as *the process of industrial mutation that continuously revolutionizes the economic structure from within, incessantly destroying the old one, incessantly creating a new one* (Schumpeter, 1942, 82–83[5]). Effectively, the Big Five and other digital winners (Uber, Airbnb, Netflix, etc.) have revolutionised their respective industries, thanks to their business models. Initially, many claimed that leaders will not be able to retain their position in the future. Certainly, if they did not adapt/reinvent their value proposition, value architecture, and value capture mechanisms– that is, their business models. However, what was true in the past may no longer be relevant today. Internet is nowadays controlled by a few players, placing barriers to disruption and the ability of insurgents to become the future giants. The concentration of power and assets tends to annihilate the possibility for newcomers (entrepreneurs) to get out from the crowd and challenge their dominant positions. This is why.

First, it is easier for newcomers to envelop their services in the ecosystems of the Big Five, instead of starting their own infrastructures from scratch.

Second, it may be less possible to find any investors ready to wait for 8 to 10 years to reach a net profit margin or a break even, as was the case in the 1990s and 2000s for some of those winners-take-all players.

Third, the battle for a critical mass requires financial resources and a strong domestic market to sustain the local critical mass. For this, the potential future giants usually come from the United States or China, as they have the sufficient size, in

---

4 "Disruptive Innovation", on Christensen Institute website, consulted in May 2022.
5 Capitalism, Socialism and Democracy, J.A. Schumpeter (1942), reedited by Routledge in 1994.

terms of unified regulation and inhabitants, to potentially sustain a traction to convince investors. Until recently and with a few exceptions, few fast-scaling European Unicorns have emerged, partially due to the complexity of the EU (languages, laws, and regulations differ from one country to the other).

Fourth, and maybe it is the main argument of a broken creative destruction engine, the Big Five have deep pockets, and as such, have the financial power to acquire nascent promising ventures whether it is for their technologies, talents, or user database. All the Big Five regularly make the headlines in the business press for their billion dollar acquisitions (WhatsApp and Instagram by Facebook; Skype and LinkedIn by Microsoft; Waze and Fitbit by Alphabet; Beats and Intel Smartphone Modem by Apple; Zapos and MGM by Amazon), but each of them has acquired more than a hundred companies along with their development and history.[6] If a large majority are related to their core business, they also use this strategy to grow and continuously enhance their ecosystem towards new sectors and consolidate their dominant position.

It is again important to dissociate services from the companies underlying them. Often, we see, as users, these services and not competitive dynamics at the level of ecosystems.

The conditions for a conducive environment changed along the way since the early 1990s. It is widely assumed that the size and savviness of the digital user, as well as an open innovation culture, can now be taken for granted. As a result, the competitive pressure is more on recruitment and retention of talent; monopoly and leadership over technology governance; and also, the ability to lobby for appropriate policies and regulations.

10.3 "Winter is Coming" or "the Future is Already Here"?

To the relatively negative picture that we have depicted above, there may be an alternative view. 'Winter is coming' means something bad is going to happen. It is a popular Game of Thrones saying. Indeed, the market dominance of digital giants is worrying. Many commentators argue that the GAFAM constitute a form of global oligopoly against public interest. As mentioned, the role of the GAFAM in the evolution of the global economy (technological convergence, deregulation, tax optimisation, etc.) as well as their grip on the potential innovation cannot be ignored. Yet, in these concluding paragraphs, we would like to propose an alternative view that epitomises the expression *The future is already here: it's just not very evenly distributed.*

Attributed to fictional writer William Gibson, this expression alludes primarily to the fact that the things that will constitute the normal or every day in the lives of

---

6 For further developments, readers can consult this article from *The Washington Post* (April 21, 2021), "How Big Tech got so big: hundreds of acquisitions", consulted in May 2022.

those living in the future already exist for some today. Today, there are more than 700 unicorns – defined as privately owned, VC-backed companies valued at $1 billion or more – around the world. They are valued at just under $2 trillion. As predicted earlier, future businesses are likely to emerge out of the USA and China. Approximately 50% of unicorns are from the United States, another 25% are now from China and the rest from the other parts of the world. Many digital giants have built their hegemony by intermediating via apps or website services that already existed: food delivery (Deliveroo), taxis (Uber), and hotels (TripAdvisor, Airbnb, Booking.com).

Unicorns are scaling at an unprecedented rate. At the start of 2016, there were 165 unicorns, and by mid-2021, there were 743, an increase of 350%. A new generation of digital companies that – at least for some – seem to be a little more sophisticated in their business model ecosystem is emerging.

First, if fintech is one of the sectors that is booming (15–20% of unicorns), other sectors are prevalent too. Software & services represent 14–18%, e-commerce (10–14%), artificial intelligence (7–10%), and the health space 6–8% . Fintech, which uses innovative technologies to automate and disintermediate financial services, is symptomatic of a platformisation that affects many sectors. Finance app platforms are now expanding beyond payments to lending, digital banking, mortgages, insurance, and wealth management. Examples include Alan, a French start-up that offers health insurance coverage for individuals and businesses. Through an app, the platform connects individuals who can send medical bills and be reimbursed almost immediately, doctors who can be reached through the app's messaging and video call services, employers who can manage sick leave. Other examples include US-based SoFi (a social lending platform) and Affirm ("buy now, pay later" or BNPL platform).

Second, environmental concerns combined with servicisation of the economy are revolutionising some traditional industries. The automotive industry, for example, is digitalising its business models to also become platform-based. US-based ChargePoint, for example, operates the largest online network of independently owned EV charging stations. These initiatives are not only backed by consumer demand and VC, but also widely supported by international organisations and national governments. The European Union has committed to invest more in green digital technologies to achieve climate neutrality and accelerate the green and digital transitions in priority sectors in Europe, by using the NextGenerationEU and InvestEU funds.

Finally, the pandemic has accelerated the emergence of new business approaches in the fields of education, gaming, and virtual meetings. As students and employees were quarantined for prolonged periods, they sought virtual options for training, personal skill development, and peer interactions. They have now changed their behaviour and continue to seek solutions for remote learning, working, gaming, and meeting. GoStudent, an Austrian-based platform now valued at €3 billion, provides paid, one-to-one, video-based tutoring to primary, secondary, and college-aged students in 30+ subjects, using a membership model. Another example is

India's BYJU'S, an education-tutoring app that runs on a freemium model, offering educational content for students who are 4 to 12 years old.

Gaming is also undergoing a substantial transformation into an environment for social connectivity and use of new technology. Dapper Labs, for example, is a consumer-focused cryptocurrency company that builds blockchain games and supports digital collectables!

Working remotely is also a big structural change that has occurred thanks to the pandemic. Remote, a Portuguese Unicorn, is considered as one of the most disruptive global payroll, tax, HR, and compliance solution. Founded in 2019, Remote targets any company with distributed teams (virtually all companies) with the mission of *opening up the world of work for every person, business, and country.*

These trends show that digitalisation of industries with the corollary need for new business models is not over. New businesses are emerging which are based on the combination of innovative technology and innovative business models. The future is already here. It is up to us to embrace, adapt to it and profit from it.

Appendices: **Illustrative Case Studies**

A The OLIO Case Study: A Social Enterprise App Tackling the "Chicken and Egg" Paradox

The Context

In December 2014, OLIO's co-founder Tessa Clarke was packing in her apartment in Switzerland to move back to the UK. Despite her best efforts, she had some leftover food in the cupboard. She desperately tried to give it away, but after hours of looking for someone who might want it, she failed (OLIO, 2020b). Thus was born the idea for OLIO – an app connecting users with each other and local businesses to share surplus food and fight food waste.

The business was officially incorporated in February 2015, with the help of co-founder Saasha Celestial-One, and the IOS and Android app launched in July. From being available in just five London postcodes, OLIO is now present in more than 60 countries, counts over 6 million users (OLIO, 2020a), raised over $50 million in five rounds of funding, and generates slightly less than £1 million in revenue each year (Table A-A)

Table A-A: OLIO Facts and Figures.

Date of app launch	July 2015
Number of active users to-date	6,000,000
Number of active businesses and ambassadors to-date	Over 50,000
Annual revenue	Over £1,000,000
Countries where the app is present	Over 60
Funding rounds	5
Total funding raised	Over $50,000,000
Portions of food saved to-date	55 million
Number of employees	85

(Source: OLIO website and email exchange with co-founder Tessa Clarke).

Business Model

By acting as an intermediary between users and businesses trying to sustainably access and dispose of excess food, OLIO fits into the category of multi-sided platforms

Note: Appendix A by Elena Cherubini

(MSP, see Figure A–A). These businesses create value by enabling direct interactions between two or more sides of the market, generally consumers and producers, with both parties benefiting from gaining access to the other side (Hagiu & Wright, 2014). MSPs also tend to have a dual-value proposition, specific to each side of the market, with the two often strictly interlinked (Muzellec, Ronteau, & Lambkin, 2015).

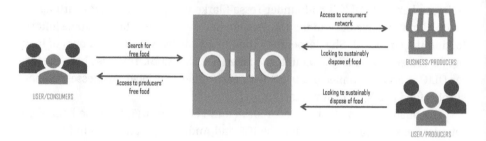

Figure A-A: OLIO's Multi-Sided Platform Model.

In OLIO's case, the platform enables consumers (users) to share leftover food as well as pick it up from their peers and/or producers (businesses). They gain value by sharing their food without wasting it, as well as receiving free goods. Businesses, on the other hand, by accessing the consumer network, get to dispose of their excess food for a flat fee, compared to the charges of a traditional waste disposal company. They also gain access to OLIO's Food Waste Heroes (volunteers), who take care of picking up and sharing the food, simplifying the process for business partners. Both sides also experience the benefit of knowing they are contributing to OLIO's mission of ending food waste (Figure A–B).

Unlike its main competitor, food-sharing app Too Good To Go, the interactions on OLIO are completely free – with the company generating revenue from the business side – and they are not limited to a B2C model but also offer the possibility of a C2C exchange.

The "Chicken and Egg" Challenge

Due to their being so co-dependent, OLIO's value propositions rely on the company's ability to generate a positive cross-side network effect, where the larger the number of consumers, the higher the value to producers and *vice versa* (Hinz, Otter, & Skiera, 2020). By scaling both sides of the market, the platform increases its attractiveness and value to both consumers and producers, encouraging increased use and sign-ups.

However, since both sides are needed to incentivise each other to join, OLIO faced what is commonly known as the "chicken and egg paradox" (Bakos & Katsamakas, 2008). To attract businesses, a platform needs a large base of registered users but, at

Customer Segment: Users (Consumers)

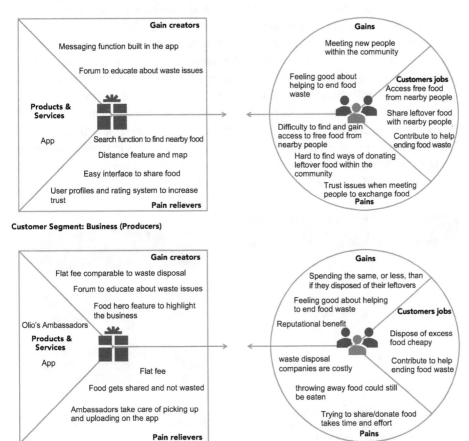

Customer Segment: Business (Producers)

Figure A-B: OLIO's Value Proposition Canvas for Users and Businesses.

the same time, users will be willing to register only if they can access products from the other side (Caillaud & Jullien, 2003). In OLIO's case, businesses will not join the platform unless there are users interested in picking up their food, but users will also not join unless there are businesses, or other users, supplying the free food. Onboarding both sides was therefore a crucial step towards sustainability for the company.

Overcoming the Challenge

To overcome the "chicken and egg" challenge and generate positive network effects, OLIO engaged in a mix of platform launch strategies and marketing techniques to seed both sides and achieve scale. It started with a very narrow focus, just five

London postcodes, to test its value proposition and iterate the product (Ajilore, 2018). This enabled it to reduce the total market size and gain loyal users who were highly committed to OLIO's mission of ending food waste.

Further, to kickstart the initial user onboarding, even with a very limited marketing budget, OLIO took advantage of the word-of-mouth power by launching an ambassador programme, recruiting volunteers to spread the word in their local communities (McMullen, 2018; OLIO, 2020d). Currently, the platform still offers many volunteering opportunities for people to collaborate with them, continuing to leverage the word-of-mouth power to further enhance its user base (OLIO, 2020c). Digitally, it is also focusing strongly on leveraging electronic word-of-mouth by using its website and email marketing techniques to encourage registered users to share the app with their networks on social media (Figure A–C).

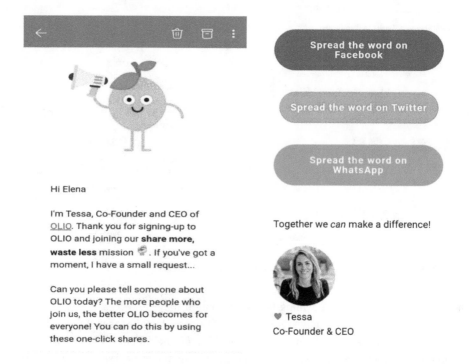

Figure A-C: OLIO's Email Marketing to Encourage e-WOM.
(Source: Screenshot of Olio email sent to account after signing up for the app)

However, the most effective strategy was what Stummers et al. (2018, 171) described as the side-switching tactic, where an MSP becomes one-sided by "finding a platform design that allows users to fill both market sides" simultaneously. OLIO's initial proposition followed this method by allowing subscribers to fulfill both the role of the end-consumer, by picking up the free leftover food, and that of the producer, by uploading and sharing their own food. This way, users would find value in the platform even without the presence of the business side, and a positive network externality would be generated, avoiding the issue of the "chicken and egg".

Of course, since OLIO offers its services to users entirely free, at this stage, despite the growing number of users, the company was still not generating revenue and could therefore not be considered a viable long-term business. However, by the end of 2017, it was able to reach enough scale on the user side – 340,000 – to interest paying businesses to join, as there was enough activity on the platform for them to perceive value in their participation. Once businesses were added in 2018, under the label of Food Waste Heroes, OLIO was able to become a revenue-generating company, while also increasing the value provided to its users by ensuring a steady supply of food to the platform.

The company took things further in 2020 with a UK-wide partnership with Tesco (Smithers, 2020), proving that once the network effects start kicking in, the app can convince even the UK's biggest supermarket (Kantar, 2020) to buy into its mission.

References

Ajilore, J. (2018) 'How Tessa Cook Is Tackling the Food Wastage Problem with OLIO, YHP, 7 March [Online]. Available at: http://yhponline.com/2018/03/07/how-tessa-cook-is-tackling-the-food-wastage-problem-with-olio/ (Accessed: 15 October 2020).

Bakos, Y. & Katsamakas, E. (2008). Design and Ownership of Two-Sided Networks: Implications for Internet Platforms. Journal of Management Information Systems, 25(2), 171–202, Business Source Complete [Online]. Available at: http://eds.b.ebscohost.com/eds/pdfviewer/pdfviewer?vid=1&sid=eb103a48-0f44-4572-8c75-3c749ea22bb5%40sessionmgr101 (Accessed: 14 October 2020).

Caillaud, B. & Jullien B. (2003). Chicken and Egg: Competition Among Intermediation Service Providers. The RAND Journal of Economics, 34(2), 309–328, JSTOR [Online]. Available at: https://www.jstor.org/stable/1593720?seq=1#metadata_info_tab_contents (Accessed: 12 October 2020).

Hagiu, A. & Wright, J. (2014). Marketplace or Reseller? Management Science, 61(1), 184–203, Informs [Online]. Available at: https://doi.org/10.1287/mnsc.2014.2042 (Accessed: 11 October 2020).

Hinz, O., Otter, T., & Skiera, B. (2020). Estimating Network Effects in Two-sided Markets. Journal of Management Information Systems, 37(1), 12–38, Taylor and Francis Online [Online]. Available at: https://www.tandfonline.com/doi/full/10.1080/07421222.2019.1705509 (Accessed: 13 October 2020).

Kantar. (2020). Great Britain Grocery Market Share. Available at: https://www.kantarworldpanel.com/en/grocery-market-share/great-britain (Accessed: 16 October 2020).

McMullan, T. (2018). OLIO's Founders on Fighting Food Waste and Funding a Startup. Alphr, 21 June [Online]. Available at: https://www.alphr.com/business/1009643/olio-fighting-food-waste-funding-startup/ (Accessed: 15 October 2020).

Muzellec, L., Ronteau, S., & Lambkin, M. (2015). Two-sided Internet Platforms: A Business Model Lifecycle Perspective. Industrial Marketing Management, 45, 139–150, Science Direct [Online].

Available at: https://www.sciencedirect.com/science/article/pii/S0019850115000474?via%
3Dihub (Accessed: 9 October 2020).

Olio. (2020a). Our Impact. Available at: https://olioex.com/about/our-impact/ (Accessed:
10 October 2020).

Olio. (2020b). Our Story. Available at: https://olioex.com/about/our-story/ (Accessed:
10 October 2020).

Olio. (2020c). Spread the Word Now. Available at: https://olioex.com/get-involved/spread-the-
word/ (Accessed: 16 October 2020).

Olio. (2020d). Volunteer. Available at: https://olioex.com/get-involved/volunteer (Accessed:
16 October 2020).

Smithers, R. (2020). Tesco to Work with Sharing App Olio in Bid to Drive Down Food Waste. The
Guardian, 17 September [Online]. Available at: https://www.theguardian.com/business/
2020/sep/17/tesco-to-work-with-sharing-app-olio-in-bid-to-drive-down-food-waste (Accessed:
16 October 2020).

Stummers, C., Kundisch, D., & Decker, R. (2018). Platform Launch Strategies. Business &
Information Systems Engineering, 60 (2), 167–173, ProQuest [Online]. Available at: https://
search.proquest.comdocview/1993347070/FBF56E9A85E64AA1PQ/6?account (Accessed:
14 October 2020).

B Amazon Versus Alibaba: Amazon is Amazing, but can Alibaba Dethrone it?

Amazon

Amazon belongs to the quartet of business giants – Google, Apple, Meta, and Amazon – collectively known as "GAMA". While Apple and Meta have relatively straightforward and well-known business models, Amazon's is more complex. Seemingly a simple e-commerce multi-sided platform, Amazon offers a variety of services and products connected through an infrastructure that is invisible to the end customer. An online retailer before becoming a multi-sided platform, now only a small part of Amazon's revenue comes from e-commerce activity.

Since its inception in 1995, Amazon did not generate yearly profit until 2003 (it reported a quarterly profit in the Q4 of 2001), eight years after it was founded. This made it appear a risky proposition, leaving founder, Jeff Bezos, struggling to find investors. Things were not helped by a lack of infrastructure to support digital business in the early days of e-commerce, as it scaled up.

To counter this problem, Amazon developed its own infrastructure by developing specific business models for different aspects of the business. For instance, in 1998, Amazon patented the "1-click" system, allowing customers to purchase an item with a single click. Until 2017 (i.e., until the patent lasted), other businesses paid a license fee to the company for using this technology. Similarly, Amazon also launched a marketplace named zShop (now renamed Amazon marketplace) in 1998 to bring third-party sellers on its platform. This, effectively, was the foundation of Amazon's emergence as a multi-sided platform.

As these matured, together they created an ecosystem that was of value to other businesses. It is this ecosystem that has enabled Amazon to move beyond being just a multi-sided e-commerce platform. In 2003, the company launched Amazon Web Services (AWSs), by licensing its platform to other businesses. The early version allowed developers to use and customise Amazon's platform for their use. By 2006, Amazon had launched cloud services in the form of AWS, which Microsoft and Google were yet to do. This provided them a head-start in the Software as a Service (SaaS) market (see Chapter 6 on sharing economy) and established them as a technology service provider. In fact, the company went a step further and launched AWS Marketplace – a multi-sided platform for software products – in 2012, thereby drawing on its expertise from the technology and platform businesses. In line with its strategy of developing the infrastructure, it also acquired a robotics company – Kiva Systems – in the same year, to automate its fulfillment centres.

Note: Appendix B by Sebastien Ronteau

In its core business, sensing the move to the digital version of books, Amazon launched Kindle in 2007 (for eBooks) and acquired Audible (for audiobooks) in 2008. This was followed by the acquisition of Twitch – a social video game streaming site – in 2014. This way, the company ventured into the bit-vendor category discussed in Section 3.2. Amazon Prime, for instance, besides targeting e-commerce customers, also provides an infrastructure for developers of applications like the Kindle Fire or Fire TV and publishing tools such as eBooks for Kindle, as well as the shipping infrastructure for Amazon Fresh.

Drawing from the long tail strategy, Amazon also acquired businesses in certain sectors to enter certain segments. For instance, after a limited presence in the shoe market, Amazon acquired Zappos, a prominent shoe shopping site with a loyal customer base, in 2009. Similarly, after struggling in the grocery delivery market, Amazon acquired Whole Foods in 2015.

Many of these business models, on their own, are not unique to Amazon. However, taken together, this constellation of business units most differentiates Amazon from other large businesses like Google, Apple, or Facebook. This enables Amazon to generate revenues not only from its marketplace and reseller activities but also in other ways. For instance, many companies in sectors from banking, social media, and travel through to entertainment, productivity and healthcare now use AWS, so much so that when in early 2017 there was an outage of AWS, 60% of the Internet was inaccessible. Such is the volume of transactions that Amazon's revenues now exceed those of Facebook and Google (Alphabet).

Amazon CEO, Jeff Bezos, says that the development of this galaxy of services and products is motivated by the desire to "sell and deliver stuff to customers". Amazon's definition of "stuff" is extensive, encompassing not only physical and digital products but also services. The company is further differentiated by its prices, which are lower than those of other physical and online merchants in what is a commoditised market.

Following the idea of a long tail, a large selection also makes Amazon a one-stop shopping destination, putting it on top of consumers' minds as a single point-of-sale for everything. The convenience of the user interface and the ergonomics of the website add to a positive user experience, which includes shipping capabilities and the company's mastery of the supply chain. In every respect, Amazon is an innovator.

For example, it uses predictive shipping to ensure local warehouses are appropriately stocked with items of interest to that area's customers. The algorithm anticipates the trends that will drive higher sales of certain items in specific locations by drawing on data from site visits, traditional media, social media influencers, social media listening, and other sources.

This means Amazon can determine that it is likely that 100 people will buy the new Dan Brown novel next week and accordingly ship 100 copies to the warehouse so that when customers push the "buy" button, their book is delivered to their doorstep within two days. This fast shipping means customers avoid the inconvenience and cost of travelling to a physical store, enabling Amazon to compete with physical retailers locally.

Amazon's strategies have been effective in changing the way customers buy and consume products. Just think about Kindle, a "digital book reader" Amazon launched despite its disrupting its own business model as an online seller of physical books. However, in creating the Kindle, Amazon was offering its consumers extra value. By working backwards from where customers like to read, Amazon solved a problem for many in urban areas who want to read while commuting to work on public transport but find hardbound books heavy, cumbersome, and taking up too much space in their bags.

With Amazon offering base-model Kindles at low, subsidised prices in anticipation of generating future sales of digital books with an inventory cost of almost zero, suddenly commuters had an inexpensive device holding thousands of books in a fraction of the space of a paperback. Moreover, if they used a Kindle app, they did not even have to buy an e-reader because they could read any digital title on the smartphone or tablet that they already owned. A publishing tipping point was reached in 2012 when on Christmas Day, Amazon's sales of digital books exceeded those of physical books.

Amazon adopted a similar strategy for B2B services. They changed the way how software was delivered – from software as a product to software as a service. While the world was still relying on on-premise technology infrastructure and software installations, Amazon launched cloud-based AWS services in 2006. Google and Microsoft could follow the suit only after a couple of years in 2008 and 2009, respectively. In this situation, it is no wonder that in 2019, one-third (33%) of the cloud market was still owned by AWS, with Microsoft being a distant second at 16% and Google with a meagre 8% of the cloud market.

In contrast, eBay largely remained an online marketplace. While it acquired PayPal – a third-party payment provider – in 2002, the latter spun off from the former in 2014. eBay's primary source of revenue is still in the form of transactions, with secondary revenue coming from marketing services (e.g., advertisements on its site). This demonstrates that eBay is a much more traditional e-commerce business than Amazon. It relies primarily on the intermediation between sellers and buyers and has not followed Amazon by selling its infrastructure/services or venturing into other domains.

Alibaba

Being the biggest eCommerce company in China, Alibaba is often compared to Amazon. However, upon closer inspection, one finds that Alibaba combines elements from Amazon, eBay, and Google, with a dash of PayPal thrown in.

The biggest share of Alibaba's business comes through TaoBao marketplace, on which Alibaba matches the buyers and sellers. In this regard, it is closer to eBay than to Amazon since Alibaba does now own an inventory and engages in direct sales. However, unlike eBay which charges the sellers for the listing, listings are free on Taobao. Instead, taking a leaf from Google's playbook, Alibaba offers marketing tools to sellers through its TaoBao marketplace. While it is free to sell on the platform, sellers must pay if they want to be visible and rank higher in searches. This strategy, which is like Google AdWords, provides the income that subsidises the platform and allows it to remain free to users.

While Amazon offers a single marketplace (disregarding AWS marketplace that is for software) for eCommerce retail, Alibaba operates several marketplaces aimed at different segments. While Taobao is geared towards the traditional retail marketplace open to any seller, TMall is a branch of Alibaba that acts as a marketplace for established international brands to access Chinese customers, while AliExpress allows Chinese manufacturers and retailers to target international consumers.

Alibaba has separate offerings in the B2B marketplace. While 1688.com is geared towards domestic B2B business, Alibaba.com aims to become a leading marketplace for global B2B business. Alibaba is also present in the B2B cloud market, with its offering Alibaba Cloud, since 2009. It is the biggest cloud service provider in China and Asia-Pacific.

Alibaba also has a payment system, named Ant Financials, which is like PayPal. However, it also acts as a bank that offers loans to small and micro businesses. This combination of Alibaba's branches creates a highly appealing galaxy of services. Perhaps not surprisingly, at its initial public offering, the biggest in US stock market history, Alibaba was valued at nearly 50% more than initial estimates. A domestic market in China of almost 1.4 billion people, approaching four times that of the US, puts Alibaba in a dominant position. Moreover, with China as a worldwide manufacturing hub, Alibaba can connect directly with manufacturers and suppliers. To exploit its potential, Alibaba has invested in what they call Cainiano Network to provide logistics services and supply chain management solutions for order fulfillment.

In terms of threats to Alibaba's growth in non-Chinese markets, protectionism may be a factor as the US moves towards policies that limit foreign companies' ability to expand into its market. However, even if Alibaba's marketplace cannot operate in the US, its banking system and financial dynamics might be able to, even if indirectly, as their social media branch, WeChat, could function as an interface through which users pay for goods and services. With its ability to combine social media, digital currencies, and mobile at a global level, Alibaba could shape global e-commerce trends in the future.

C BlaBlaCar: Value Creation on a Digital Platform

Abstract: From its humble origin in 2003, BlaBlaCar has become a preferred ride-sharing platform for passengers across Europe. BlaBlaCar is an online marketplace that connects drivers and passengers and helps them share the costs of journeys. In the process, it creates value for both sides of the platform. Drivers save money on the cost of the trip, and passengers get a low-cost option to reach their destination. The case follows the company from the idea to its inception to its growth and current challenges. The case helps the students in understanding the business of digital platforms, as it relates to value creation for the customers, matching the value proposition for two sides, revenue and pricing strategies, and the crucial role of trust in sharing economy.

Introduction

On April 24, 2018, the trains in France were on strike (again). For the international press, strikes are an opportunity to mock French labour laws or praise workers' *esprit de corps* in defending their rights. For commuters, however, strikes are neither a laughable matter nor a source of pride. Strikes have practical implications for commuters that include being stranded, missing work or a family reunion, getting a much longer commute, or squeezing into one of the few trains that are still running. However, over the last few years, an Internet platform has considerably contributed to minimising the inconvenience caused by such events to commuters: BlaBlaCar.

BlaBlaCar is an online marketplace that connects drivers and passengers and helps them share the costs of journeys. On April 24, 2018, Fred plays the role of a driver and takes on board a retired couple who were using BlaBlaCar for the first time. He listens to their complaints about the railroad service but also the difficulties they encountered when signing up on BlaBlaCar. As they did not have a Facebook account, they created one before they could sign up on the platform. It took them a while to complete all the formalities. In the end, they are delighted to be in the car with Fred, on their way to see their grandchildren. Fred listens carefully and thinks of the solutions that could improve their experience. This is because Fred is no ordinary member of the BlaBlaCar community. In fact, Fred is the founder of the company. He uses every trip as an opportunity to understand consumers' needs and concerns better and think of solutions and/or innovations.

Note: Appendix C by Deepak Saxena, Laurent Muzellec, and Daniel Trabucchi. Originally published in Journal of Information Technology Teaching Cases, 10(2), 2020.

How the Idea was Born

Around 15 years ago in December 2003, Fred Mazella was trying to go to his home-town in the Vendée region (west of France), 500 km from Paris, to spend Christmas with his family. All trains were fully booked, and no seats were available until after Christmas. Eventually, he managed to convince his sister to pick him up from Paris, a major detour for the sibling who lived in Normandy. As he was driving with her on the highway, he saw a train that he wanted to take. It was indeed overbooked with all seats occupied. At the same time, whizzing past his car were hundreds of cars that were mostly empty except for the drivers. It was a eureka moment! Fred thought, "Oh my God, there are seats for going to Vendee, but they are not on trains. They are on cars!" He wondered about a platform that could enable people who did not have cars to get lifts and drivers to find passengers who would share the cost of trips. He spent the next few days doing an online search for platforms connecting passengers and drivers. However, all he could find were some fairly confidential forums that were so unorganised that finding someone who was taking the same trip at the same time was practically impossible. His research convinced him of two things. First, the need for such types of services indeed existed, and he was not the only one in France in need of a ride to go home; in fact, a small community of users had started to emerge through those forums. Second, what was really needed was a platform equipped with a powerful algorithm that could match passengers and drivers based on the date of departure, the point of departure, and the point of arrival.

For the next three years, Fred would spend his time coding for the platform with two school friends, now engineers. When not coding, Fred would go to weekly entrepreneurial meetups to discuss his ideas and gain feedback. It was in one such forum that he met Francis Nappez, a technology expert, who offered his services if Fred decided to use the mobile platform. Soon realising his lack of skills in market-ing, management, and product development, Fred enrolled in an MBA course at IN-SEAD. During his MBA, Fred not only learned about the best business practices but also tested and refined several business models for his idea. It was at INSEAD that he met Nicolas Brusson, who was immensely interested in the venture capital world and start-up ecosystem. In 2006, Fred purchased the domain name Covoiturage.fr (French for "car sharing") and along with Nicolas and Francis (see Appendix 1 for a brief bio of founders) founded a company called Comuto.[1] Fred realised that the reason why car sharing had not fully taken off earlier was not because of the lack of interest from the potential users but rather because no platform had successfully managed to match passengers and drivers using the date and time of departure, travel origin, and travel destination. Now, Fred had a working platform that offered

---

1 Until April 2012, "Commuto" was the brand name used in Spain, and until 2013, "Covoiturage" was the brand name used in France.

the best possible solution based on the three variables. With a working platform and tentative business model, it was now time to market the services to a wider audience. Although the company had rapidly become the market leader in France, it required the final impetus to become a household name.

Seizing the Opportunities and Facing Scaling Challenges

In October 2007, Fred's sister Helene saw an opportunity and immediately called Fred. "Next week there's going to be a train strike", she said over the phone, "You've got to own this moment and send out a press release!" What seemed a normal Sunday afternoon in October 2007 suddenly turned into an all-night workshop for the siblings. As a communications expert, Helene helped Fred craft a message that portrayed BlaBlaCar as a travel option during the strikes and advised him to send the press release out first thing on Monday morning.

Merely 30 min after sending the press release, Reuters and AFP picked up the news and circulated it. Within seconds, Fred's phone began ringing continuously, and he could not sleep for the next 48 h. He ended up being on the TV and radio, and the platform was featured in over 500 newspaper articles. It was massive publicity, and for the first time, BlaBlaCar was thrown into the limelight. The fact that the platform was available on mobile to help everybody find alternative transport options during the train strikes was significant. As Fred was approached by many media outlets, Francis and the rest of the team were working full throttle behind the scenes. Owing to the increase in traffic, they made continuous changes in the code to adapt to the new volumes. The first version of the platform could handle only up to 100,000 members. When Francis formally joined the company full-time in 2008, he modified the platform architecture to accommodate another 5 million members. They continued to modify the platform to support further user growth. The platform was now on the radar of French media and would soon become a recurring topic every time there was a strike, which was indeed frequent (see Appendix 2).

The train strikes of 2007 helped BlaBlaCar become a household name in France. But now, it was time to think big and grow internationally. Once again, a shot in the arm came from an unexpected event. An Icelandic volcano started erupting on April 14, 2010, and ejected a significant amount of volcanic ash into the atmosphere, creating a potential hazard for aeroplanes. For the next six days, as the ash diffused the European airspace, fleets of airlines remained stationary, leaving approximately 10 million passengers stranded at European airports. BlaBlaCar again became a preferred solution for people stranded far from home and, in one case, for a bride who had to reach the wedding venue. Frequent strikes in France further helped the company expand its market base.

However, while such strikes and disruptions are treated as "gold dust" by the company, the platform business has its own share of complications. The main issue with such platforms is the ability to attract both sides of the market simultaneously. For the platform to be successful, both groups of customers – the consumers (passengers) and the producers (drivers) – need to be on the network. One group will not come to the network unless the other does and *vice versa*. This situation is commonly known as the "chicken and egg paradox". In the case of BlaBlaCar, passengers and drivers are the two groups of customers. While the passengers join the platform to search for rides offered by drivers, drivers search for passengers to share their travel costs. BlaBlaCar offers a service to both. Train strikes constitute a wonderful opportunity to advertise the services to both sides of the network, but the company may face problems balancing the supply with the demand.

Fred recalls that while the number of passengers was growing rapidly, enough drivers were not available to offer rides. This problem was especially acute during strikes, as they brought more passengers than drivers. After considerable contemplation, Fred and his team found a solution to the problem: emotional marketing. In this regard, Fred recounts, "During a train strike, we started just calling for drivers, asking for solidarity with passengers, saying 'Ok, trains are on strike, lots of passengers will be without a way to move around, please drivers if you have empty seats propose your seats because there are plenty of passengers searching for a ride'". The messages were available across various marketing channels from the press to social media. The notion of solidarity hit a chord with the drivers in those difficult moments.

Experimenting with Business Models

Interestingly, while the company made strides in terms of its user base and there was no dearth of venture capital (see Appendix 3), it struggled to find the right business segment and pricing model. The idea of a carpooling platform had the potential for both individual and business consumers. Back in 2007, the company received many requests from businesses and local authorities in France interested in integrating a carpooling platform with their corporate intranet. Their main focus was facilitating homework travel over short distances (usually less than 20 km). While this purpose was not aligned with Fred's original idea of long-distance travel (averaging 300 km) between cities, it still was a lucrative option to customise the platform for other businesses. Carrefour, IKEA, and some hospitals in Marseille were among the first to integrate the platform within their portal. Over the years, around 200 companies utilised the service. In 2009, BlaBlaCar earned approximately €10k per month from the sales of their platforms to businesses. Although it was a steady source of revenue for BlaBlaCar, it required investing considerable time, resources, and attention to deliver such multiple customised platforms to various companies. Another issue for the company was that the solution was not scalable due to the differing requirements of customers. Over time, it became clear to Fred and his team that the business-to-business

(B2B) model would not flourish. Eventually, the decision to phase out the B2B model was taken in 2012.

The closure of the B2B platform service allowed the company to exclusively focus on the C2B2C (or B2C&C) model, where the platform would enable transactions between the two sides of a market. Two-sided markets are economic platforms having two distinct user groups that provide each other with network benefits. In the case of BlaBlaCar, the two sides are the passengers and the drivers. They benefit from and provide economic benefits to each other. The drivers can subsidise the costs of their trips by sharing the costs of travel.[2] The passenger(s) also benefit from reduced prices as well as increased flexibility compared to the time, pick up, and destination options available through public transport. The network benefits are known as cross-side network externalities. This means that the value of the platform for the passengers depends on the rides offered by the drivers, and at the same time, the value for the drivers depends on the passengers asking for rides.

Within this model, however, BlaBlaCar still needed to figure out its revenue and pricing scheme. For some time, a freemium model was adopted, in which the overall service remained free, and the members had the option to pay for additional services. By paying a monthly or annual fee, the premium members could have the benefit of having their posts ranked higher in search engines and receiving text messages each time they had a request. However, upon further deliberation, it was understood that the option was not fair to other consumers. The team also deemed the option to be financially unviable in the long run. Implementing a monthly subscription plan with a flat fee was also considered. However, the subscription idea was also quickly discarded because of the uneven use of the platform. While some members used the platform sporadically (a few times per year), some others used it frequently (several times a week). Consequently, it was impossible to devise a subscription formula that was fair to all. BlaBlaCar also tested the advertising model as the majority of the internet service providers do. However, there were concerns within the team about the possibility of the misuse of the personal data of members by the affiliates for commercial purposes. It was also antithetical to the philosophy of trust (see the next section) that the company followed. Consequently, the company decided not to follow the advertising route, to protect the personal data of their members.

Currently, the pricing and revenue model differs from country to country (see Appendix 4). For instance, the platform is free in the markets that it is penetrating. With this strategy, the company has entered Eastern Europe including Russia, South America, and India. In the matured markets, however, the company follows transaction-based pricing with the passengers paying the transaction fee. Drivers get the price they ask for, but the passengers pay a slightly higher price to cover the

---

2 Drivers are supposed to cover only their fuel and road toll costs but not make a profit from the passengers.

transaction costs. In other words, one of the two sides pays the platform for both, while BlaBlaCar offers a service that matches the two sides (see Figure C-A). Fred acknowledges the difficulties associated with the transactional model: "The hardest one is the one (business model) we have, which is transactional, taking care of the money and their transfer. Moving money from a million passengers to a million drivers. And in some cases, you also have to give the money back because the transaction does not happen, and in some cases managing issues between the two."

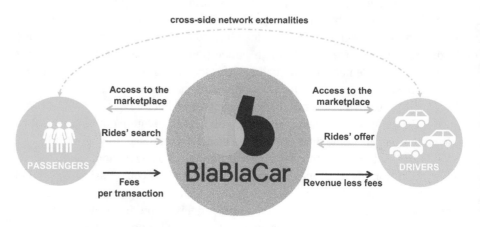

Figure C-A: BlaBlaCar as a Two-Sided Platform.

Managing Trust and Expectations

Gaining consumer trust is crucial for any business for its long-term survival. In fact, for a C2B2C platform like BlaBlaCar, it is their raison d'être. Most of the commuters would not have met before, which is why they would be using the services of BlaBlaCar in the first place. Establishing trust and rapport traditionally takes time and repeated interactions. In the beginning, the lack of trust was related to many dimensions, from getting into the car with a stranger to the actual chance of finding the passenger at the meeting point or the driver arriving at the defined meeting point. Indeed, overbooking and no show were concerns for the company in the beginning. The drivers overbooked due to the fear of no-shows. The passengers overbooked because they were unsure whether they would get a ride with the driver they booked. This resulted in a vicious circle of overbooking and cancellations with the rate of cancellation peaking at 35%.

To tackle the issues of overbooking and no-show, the company employed the following strategies. First, the company tried a bidirectional rating system. This worked well for the drivers who saw an increase in their ratings. However, it did not exactly work for the passengers. The passengers with bad feedback would book drivers with good ratings but then would not show up. The rating system resulted in penalising good drivers with unreliable passengers, which led to good drivers leaving the platform. To avoid this situation, the company asked users to pay up-front if they wanted to book a ride. Once the advance payment method was introduced, the number of cancellations plummeted to 3%.

Over the years, the company's user interface has evolved to create and manage the trust ecosystem using the six pillars of online trust (see Figure C-B) to gain "trust capital". It encourages its users to make an online trust profile based on verified information, declarative content, and others' ratings from previous experiences. Over the years, more trust features were introduced to create a trust ecosystem. It was found that members with public profile pictures and social network activities were trusted more. Based on this, the platform allows its users to log in through their Facebook accounts, instantly utilising the trust capital built through another platform. After each journey, both the passengers and drivers are encouraged to leave reviews of each other. To ensure that fair and honest ratings are given and discourage "revenge ratings", the team introduced a feature that allows members to view the rating they received only if they rate their co-travellers within 14 days.

However, the emphasis on trust goes beyond the user interface and forms the backbone of the company's operations. Back in 2012, Fred spoke at a TED event where, to the utter surprise of his audience, he tore off his shirt to unveil an orange-green emblem declaring him as Trustman. At the same time, the other members of the team sitting with the audience also unveiled themselves as Trustmen and Trustwomen.

Going beyond symbolism, BlaBlaCar teamed up with Prof. Arun Sundararajan, a sharing economy expert with NYU Stern School of Business, to conduct a continent-wide study on online trust with over 18,000 BlaBlaCar customers across 11 EU countries. To ensure that the results were unbiased and trustworthy, BlaBlaCar decided not to sponsor the research but only provide access to their customers. The results of the survey indicate that, in general, people trust members with a full BlaBlaCar profile more than a colleague. In fact, the survey indicates that the level of trust in a BlaBlaCar member is second only to the trust in family and friends. Around 70% of the users declared that so many drivers and passengers being on the platform makes them feel more comfortable ridesharing with BlaBlaCar.

Apart from trust, the comfort of co-passengers is also a significant factor when sharing a long ride with somebody. To accommodate this, BlaBlaCar introduced preference settings for members to rate themselves on parameters such as smoking preferences or chattiness. For example, while some passengers like to chat a lot with fellow passengers during a journey, some others may prefer to keep the chatter to a minimum and enjoy the scenery. Aligned with the company's name, members can rate themselves Bla, BlaBla, or BlaBlaBla, with the last one denoting the chattiest. This emphasises that the social nature of the BlaBlaCar community adds additional value, where a rideshare is not just a means to decrease the cost of travel but also an avenue that may help in forging long-term social relations based on one's conversation

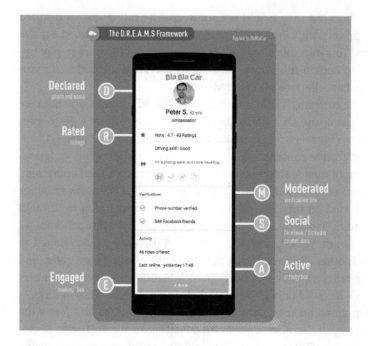

Figure C-B: The D.R.E.A.M.S Framework for Trust.

preferences. Later, the company also introduced verification information based on members' experience level, declared preferences, the inclusion of profile photos, the percentage of positive ratings received, and their seniority in terms of usage. In the order of reputation and trustworthiness, the experience levels are newcomer, intermediate, experienced, expert, and ambassador. Beyond trust, it also makes economic sense to the members, as ambassadors find it much easier to get their cars quickly filled. Ambassadors are also invited to focus groups where they provide feedback on the new features to be launched. To encourage more participation from members, recently, the company introduced a peer-to-peer chat of helpers (ambassadors who meet certain criteria) to support other members. These helpers work in direct contact with the company teams.

Challenges and Legal Issues

As BlaBlaCar grows both in size and geographical footprint, it also faces diverse challenges. It is finding it difficult to sustain itself in some markets, for example, far off in India, Mexico, Turkey, and closer in the UK. Interestingly, in most of the non-European markets, trust is a major issue. In India, for example, people usually travel long distances with friends and family and do not trust strangers to share a ride. To tackle this cultural roadblock, BlaBlaCar introduced Government ID verification, which requires members to be verified based on existing government IDs. The company planned to introduce it in Mexico and Turkey as well. However, the company failed to get a significant amount of traction for its services and had to close down local offices. The local websites are still operational, though mostly working on autopilot. BlaBlaCar is still operational in the UK and follows the government ID verification scheme, but Nicolas Brusson (co-founder and CEO) admits that BlaBlaCar "sort of works but it's nothing exciting" in the UK. In recent years, the team has also noted the limitations of geographical expansion as a growth strategy.

Closer to home in Germany, a country very fond of carpooling, BlaBlaCar is looking for the right monetisation strategy. The Germans, who prefer cash payments, are reluctant to go through the app to book trips and pay a commission in passing. In Spain, a lawsuit was filed in 2015 by the Spanish Confederation for Bus Transport (Confebus) against the company on the grounds that BlaBlaCar was in effect providing the services of a transport company and that was unfair competition. BlaBlaCar eventually won the case in 2017 based on the argument that it is not a transport company but a broker that brings drivers and passengers together to share the costs of trips and in the process earns money by charging a fee.

Despite its consistent focus on trust, BlaBlaCar is facing certain issues on the customer front. In most of its markets, its existing model is primarily based on the information supplied by the users, which has resulted in its being entangled in some legal cases and attracting bad press. A driver in France was arrested in 2014 and later sentenced in 2017, for drugging and sexually assaulting the passengers contacted through the BlaBlaCar platform. In September 2018, an Italian driver was arrested on the French-Italian border because he unknowingly shared the ride with two undocumented immigrants from Paris. The company maintains that the drivers should check their passengers' papers before starting a trip across the border. However, sceptics question the efficacy of this solution, as passengers could also be carrying prohibited substances or illegal items in their bags. Even if it is not a direct responsibility of the company, it puts a dent in the BlaBlaCar trusted ecosystem, which it is proud of so far.

The Journey Continues

Luckily, on April 24, 2018, Fred is on a domestic trip, and his elderly passengers are gentle and kind. Before dropping them off at their destination, he informs them that they could also use their e-mail to access the services of the platform and de-link their Facebook account if they wish to. As he waves them goodbye and drives home, he cannot stop thinking about what lies ahead. The company has existing plans for new revenue streams. Remaining close to its origin, the company is experimenting in France with a new offering. In April 2017, BlaBlaCar announced its partnership with the car manufacturer Opel and the long-term car rental specialist ALD Automotive that would enable its more than 300,000 French ambassador-level members to rent Opel cars on long-term rentals for a year or more. The move is to encourage its members to shift from the traditional car ownership model to a "car-as-a-service" model. Within a month, in May 2017, BlaBlaCar also offered its new platform called BlaBlaLines on two short routes in France – Reims to Châlons-en-Champagne (45 km) and Toulouse to Montauban (50 km) – to fulfil the daily commuting needs of its members. The service, which was rebranded as BlaBlaCar Daily is now growing rapidly due to the rise in gas prices and the corollary incentive to share daily commute costs. The future looks both challenging and exciting for BlaBlaCar.

Questions

1. How does BlaBlaCar create value? What is (are) the value proposition(s) of BlaBlaCar? How does it differ from other traditional businesses?
2. Explain the "chicken and egg" paradox in the context of the platform business. How did BlaBlaCar manage to overcome this paradox?
3. Do you think BlaBlaCar is correct in using different pricing models in different markets? Why or why not?
4. Explain the importance of "trust capital" in the context of C2B2C markets. Suggest ways for maintaining trust in the wake of recent events described in the case.

D Hubspot: A Complex Subscription Model for Inbound Marketing

HubSpot offers subscription-based SaaS solutions for inbound marketing, sales, and customer service. As opposed to outbound marketing, in which marketers try to reach the customers via advertisements or e-mails, inbound marketing creates content, such as blogs or information videos that interested customers would want to see. The solution offered by the company offers tools to create high-quality content, increase exposure to interested customers, and tools to analyse the results. It also offers tools to qualify the leads and close the sale on its platform.

After initially contemplating a product-based and SaaS model for different customer segments, the adoption of subscription-based SaaS delivery seemed the right strategy for HubSpot from a long-term value creation perspective. However, soon they found two distinct segments among their subscribers. While the marketers from the big firms continued with their subscription and continued to extract value, small firm owners cancelled the subscription after gaining initial value from the offerings. It was crucial to reduce the churn rate for the subscription-based business model to be viable for the company. To manage the churn rate, HubSpot made a conscious choice of avoiding signing up the customers who would possibly renege. The sales team's incentive was determined based on the retention of the customers. Moreover, the company focussed on continuously improving its onboarding and customer support process, including dedicated help centres, a knowledge base portal, and certification programs. These steps resulted in lower churn rates for the company.

HubSpot currently offers all its services on a subscription-based model with a SaaS delivery. Instead of paying upfront to install and use software, HubSpot's customers subscribe to the solutions by paying a monthly/annual fee. HubSpot follows a tiered subscription model. Some basic CRM and marketing functionality are available free of cost, followed by a starter, professional, and enterprise solutions. The subscription tiers are offered in three distinct yet inter-related areas of marketing, sales, and customer service. The subscription tiers differ in terms of the number of users supported and additional features for the subscribers (see Table A for subscription tiers and indicative features for the marketing function).

While Table D-A is not exhaustive (e.g., there are more features offered in the professional and enterprise packages), it is clear from the table that the company offers distinct value addition across subscription tiers, especially to those opting for professional or enterprise packages. The success of HubSpot's multi-tier subscription pricing strategy may be gauged from the fact that out of their total revenue of $674.9 million in 2019, around 95% ($646.3 million) was earned as subscription revenue.

Note: Appendix D by Deepak Saxena

Table D-A: HubSpot Subscription Tiers for Marketing Function.

Features	Free	Starter	Professional	Enterprise
			Plans	
Pricing	–	Starting at €36.80 per month / €441.60 per year	Starting at €740 per month /€8,880 per year	Starting at €2,944 per month / €35,328 per year
Contacts included	–	1,000	1,000	10,000
Email marketing	2,000 email sends per calendar month	5X contact tier email send limit	10X contact tier email send limit per calendar month	10X contact tier email send limit per calendar month
Ad management	$1k spend limit Simple website audiences only	$1k spend limit 2 contact list audiences	$10k spend limit 5 audiences	$30k spend limit 15 audiences
List segmentation	5 smart lists, 25 static lists	25 smart lists, 25 static lists	1,000 smart lists 1,000 static lists	1,500 smart lists 1,500 static lists
Conversations inbox	1	1	100	100
Reporting dashboards	3	3	5	25
Custom properties	10	1,000	1,000	1,000
Ad retargeting	None	All available ad types $1k spend limit 2 audiences	All available ad types $10k spend limit 5 audiences	All available ad types $30k spend limit 15 audiences
Multiple currencies	None	5 currencies	30 currencies	200 currencies
Social media			50 connected accounts for social media 10,000 posts per month	300 connected accounts for social media 10,000 posts per month
Subdomain availability			1 subdomain	Unlimited subdomains
Marketing automation			300 workflows	1,000 workflows
Custom reports			20	500

(Source: HubSpot)

E AirBnB: Managing Trust and Safety on a Platform Business

Abstract: AirBnB has become a preferred accommodation marketplace for travellers worldwide. AirBnB is a two-sided digital platform that connects guests and hosts. In the process, it creates value for both sides of the platform. Guests save money on the accommodation and hosts generate earnings from their otherwise idle space. The case follows the company from its inception to its growth and current challenges with the wider community. The case enables understanding the key features of digital platforms: how they create value for all users, how they shape value propositions for two sides, and how the community becomes a stakeholder in the platform business. It also focuses on the issue of trust and the need for the company to integrate the concerns of other stakeholders such as communities and local authorities. Finally, the case highlights the impact of Covid-19 on the company and the travel industry.

Keywords: digital platform, multisided platform, value proposition, business model, trust

Introduction

AirBnB is a digital accommodation marketplace providing access to 7 million places of stay in more than 100,000 cities and 220 countries/regions globally.[1] It does this by connecting the owners of accommodations (referred to as hosts) with customers (guests) who would like to use this accommodation on their travels. The company had been experiencing exponential growth since its inception in 2007. However, in recent years, it has started experiencing some difficulties. For example, during the autumn of 2017, five people died in a shooting incident during a Halloween party in Orinda, California. The property was rented using the AirBnB platform. This reflects a growing discontent of the community in AirBnB hotspots. The company has faced lawsuits in France, its biggest market outside the US. In Ireland, AirBnB is blamed for a reduction in the supplies of long-term rentals in Dublin, thereby fuelling the housing crisis. Such incidents started to put a question mark on the trust ecosystem that the company has built over the years. Yet, these criticisms were small waves, compared to the tempest around the corner. In the spring of 2020, the covid-19 pandemic took the world by surprise. To slow down the spread of the virus, governments across

---

1 Source: AirBnB.com; Available at https://news.airbnb.com/fast-facts/.

Note: Appendix E by Caoimhe Walsh, Deepak Saxena, and Laurent Muzellec. Originally published in *The Irish Journal of Management*, Sciendo, 39(2).

the world imposed travel restrictions. This practically annihilated all AirBnB revenue until the beginning of summer 2020. In the words of the AirBnB CEO, the pandemic presents a 'prolonged storm' for travel. Consequently, on May 5, AirBnB announced that it was getting rid of one-fourth of its workforce, which is about 1,900 employees. The Covid-19 pandemic meant that AirBnB had to review its marketing strategy or even reinvent its business model, which reinvented the accommodation marketplace in the first place.

Starting the Business

AirBnB's saga began in 2007, when Brian Chesky and Joe Gebbia (see Appendix 1 for a brief bio of co-founders), both graduates of the Rhode Island School of Design, having moved from New York to San Francisco, were unemployed and having trouble paying their rent (see Appendix 2 for AirBnB's journey). It came to their attention that all the hotel rooms in the city were booked out due to a local industrial design conference. They saw the opportunity to make some money by renting out some of the space they had in their apartment. They bought some airbeds and quickly set up a simple website called Air Bed & Breakfast. Their first guests were a 30-year-old Indian man, a 35-year-old woman from Boston, and a 45-year-old father of four from Utah. They charged each of them $80 a night. Shortly after this beginning, Nathan Blecharczyk, a Harvard graduate, and technical architect joined the team as the third co-founder and chief technical officer.

While the founders initially found it difficult to attract investors to their new venture, in 2009, they raised $20,000 from their first investor, Y Combinator. They used this money to fly to New York City, their biggest market at the time, to meet users and promote the business. They found that a key problem was that the photos of the accommodations were not of good quality. They bought a high-quality camera and visited each accommodation, taking new photographs for the website. Returning to San Francisco with a more viable business model, they shortened the name to AirBnB.com and expanded their offering from just airbeds and shared accommodation to a range of properties from entire homes and apartments to private rooms. By March 2009, the site had 10,000 users and 2,500 listings.

AirBnB's business model is referred to as a two-sided (more specifically, C2B2C) digital platform, matching the guests (travellers) with the hosts (property owners). In so doing, it creates value for both sides of the platform. Guests save money on the accommodation (compared to hotels), and hosts get earnings from their otherwise idle space. The company has a simple revenue model. There is no charge for the hosts to list their accommodation on the website. When guests book a property, AirBnB receives its revenue from two sources. First, it charges a flat 10% commission from hosts for every booking made through the platform. Second, it charges 3% of the booking amount as a transaction fee from guests on every confirmed booking.

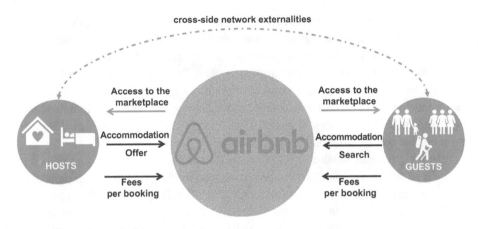

Figure E-A: AirBnB as a Two-Sided Platform.

Business Expansion

In November 2010, AirBnB launched its iPhone app along with an Instant Book feature that enables bookings without the host's prior approval. The following year, they opened an office in Germany, which marked the beginning of their international expansion. In May 2012, AirBnB introduced its $1 m Host Guarantee, which provided property damage protection of up to $1 m for every host at no extra cost. In 2014, the company hosted more than 100,000 guests during the Rio World Cup and relaunched their brand. Over the following three years, AirBnB held open events in San Francisco, Paris, and Los Angeles with the number of hosts attending growing from 1,500 to 7,000.

To add value to the customers, in 2016, AirBnB announced the launch of Trips,[2] which expanded its services beyond accommodation to local experiences recommended by hosts. With Trips, they also introduced a new identity authentication process that requires hosts and guests to provide an official government ID and a separate photograph that is matched to the authenticated ID. AirBnB notes that this more robust standard of authenticating identity made their community stronger and reaffirms their commitment to authenticity, reliability, and security. In 2017, AirBnB expanded the Trips services to 20 more cities globally and launched its Chinese brand. The following year, AirBnB introduced a new accommodation category AirBnB Plus, which recognises exceptionally high quality and comfort, at an extra

---

2 Source: AirBnB.com; Available at https://news.airbnb.com/airbnb-expands-beyond-the-home-with-the-launch-of-trips/.

charge of $149 per host. In 2019, AirBnB signed an agreement to acquire HotelTo-night,[3] an online app that allows users to find discounted last-minute hotel accom-modation. This makes it easier for people who use AirBnB to find last-minute places to stay when home hosts are often already booked. This, together with the Trips ser-vice, further expanded AirBnB's range of offerings for its customers. From its humble beginnings in 2007, AirBnB now connects travellers to more than 7 million places to stay and tens of thousands of experiences around the world. It is now the most searched for accommodations brand on Google.

To fund their expansion, AirBnB raised $4.7 billion in total funding across 10 funding rounds (see Appendix 3 for more details on funding rounds). To undertake an initial public offering, the business was valued at $31 billion at the beginning of 2020. In the last six years alone, in its key US market, it has seen substantial gains in sales vis-à-vis key industry competitors and similar gains in market share. Its yearly reve-nue has increased from $8.4 billion in 2010 to $3.6 billion in 2018 (see Appendix 4 for yearly figures). In 2018, its sales surpassed the Hilton group, and it is also gaining on the Marriott hotel chain. On March 27, 2019, the company celebrated a key milestone, with the announcement that since its founding in 2007, half a billion guests had checked in at AirBnB listings worldwide.[4] In May 2019, the company announced that it had added 1 million new listings since July 2018, while in the same period, Marriott had added 46,101 new rooms.[5] In August 2019, Reuters reported that AirBnB had re-corded $9.4 billion in total booking value in the first quarter, corresponding to a book-ing of 91 million nights on its platform in the same quarter.[6]

Breaches of Trust

While in the initial years, multiple bookings and stranded hosts were key issues, in recent years, several cases were reported in which guests have discovered hidden cameras in their accommodation. One recent case occurred in Cork city in Ireland in April 2019.[7] A family from New Zealand found a camera hidden in a smoke alarm in the living room. The father of the family, an IT consultant, discovered the camera

---

3 Source: AirBnB.com; Available at https://news.airbnb.com/airbnb-signs-agreement-to-acquire-hoteltonight/.
4 Source: AirBnB.com; Available at https://press.airbnb.com/airbnb-celebrates-half-a-billion-guest-arrivals/.
5 Source: AirBnB.com; Available at https://press.airbnb.com/airbnbs-growth-and-summer-travel-updates/.
6 Source: Reuters.com; Available at https://www.reuters.com/article/us-airbnb-results/airbnb-re cords-30-growth-rate-in-first-quarter-on-booking-strength-source-idUSKCN1V700L.
7 Source: Irish Times; Available at https://www.irishtimes.com/news/consumer/family-felt-sense-of-danger-after-finding-hidden-live-cam-in-cork-airbnb-1.3850498.

after trying to connect his phone to the Wi-Fi. He found a link to a device that enabled him to watch a live video stream on his phone. His wife Ms. Barker said, "We felt a sense of danger the moment we discovered the camera. It felt like a huge invasion of our privacy, and it felt like the exact opposite of what AirBnB should be about – mutual trust." The family was very disappointed and upset with how AirBnB handled the investigation initially. They felt they had to chase the company to get answers and even when the listing was removed from the platform, they were not informed by AirBnB. The Cork city hidden camera incident is not an isolated one. Similar cases were reported in Miami, Florida, California, and Bulgaria, covered widely in the international press.

A spokesman for AirBnB responded in a press statement:

> We have permanently removed this bad actor from our platform. Our original handling of this incident did not meet the high standards we set for ourselves, and we have apologized to the family and fully refunded their stay. The safety and privacy of our community – both online and offline – is our priority. AirBnB policies strictly prohibit hidden cameras in listings, and we take reports of any violations extremely seriously. There have been more than 500 million guest arrivals in AirBnB listings to date and negative incidents are incredibly rare.

Ensuring Trust and Safety

AirBnB indeed realises trust and safety are central to their platform, as noted by Joe Gebbia in his 2016 TED talk. AirBnB has a 'Trust & Safety' team that deals with travelling, hosting, community standards and home safety. A study[8] conducted jointly with Stanford University found that strong reputational mechanisms on the platform can overcome bias and boost trust. It employs three reputational mechanisms to help its users overcome the anxiety associated with dealing with strangers:

Profile: Guests and hosts on AirBnB need to create a profile for using the platform. A basic profile includes fields such as full name, phone number, payment information, and email address. The hosts also need to provide photographs of the accommodation.

Secure messaging: The platform provides a secure messaging tool for communication between the guest and the host. The two parties may use the tool for sharing additional information/requests and for coordination.

Reviews: The reviews, in which the guests and hosts can review each other after the reservation, arguably provide the strongest reputational mechanism on AirBnB. The

---

8 Abrahao, B., Parigi, P., Gupta, A., & Cook, K. S. (2017). Reputation Offsets Trust Judgments based on Social Biases among AirBnB Users. Proceedings of the National Academy of Sciences, 114(37), 9848–9853.

Stanford study found the rating system and textual reviews to be strong mechanisms for maintaining trust.

To boost its trust ecosystem, AirBnB started a superhost programme in which exceptional hosts are eligible for a 'superhost' status, based on the following criteria – average rating of 4.8 or above out of 5, having completed at least 10 stays (or 100 nights over the last 3 completed stays) over the last year, less than 1% cancellation rate, and more than 90% response rate. Superhosts get benefits in the form of getting featured on the platform, attracting more hosts, and receiving an additional bonus from the platform. There are around 400,000 superhosts on the AirBnB platform, around 10% of the overall number of hosts.

Moreover, to enhance the trust and safety of its platform, AirBnB provides the following features:

Account protection: AirBnB employs multifactor authentication on its platform, whenever there is an attempt to log in from a new device or location. It also sends alerts whenever there is any change in the account or the transaction.

Scam prevention: AirBnB provides multilayer defence mechanisms against scams. As long as the users stay on and communicate within the platform, they are protected from scams.

Secure payments: AirBnB transfers payments through its own platform and discourages users from paying via other means such as wire transfers or cash, which are outside the platform. This helps to ensure the traceability and security of the transactions.

Risk scoring: AirBnB scores each reservation for potential risk based on machine learning and predictive analytics. The scores are based on hundreds of flags derived from past transactions.

Watchlists and background checks: AirBnB also regularly checks its hosts and guests against sanctions, regulatory, and terrorist watchlists. It also conducts its own background checks for its US customers.

Home preparedness: AirBnB runs home safety workshops for the hosts, in conjunction with local experts. The hosts are supposed to provide important local information to the guests. The company also provides free smoke and/or carbon monoxide detectors to the hosts if they wish. Regarding hidden cameras, their policy[9] for hosts clearly states:

---

9 Source: AirBnB.com; Available at https://www.airbnb.ie/help/article/887/what-are-airbnbs-rules-about-security-cameras-and-other-recording-devices-in-listings.

You should not spy on other people; cameras are not allowed in your listing unless they are previously disclosed and visible, and they are never permitted in private spaces (such as bathrooms or sleeping areas).

From Two-Sided to a Multisided Platform?

However, with time, AirBnB's trust and safety concerns have expanded beyond the two sides–hosts and guests–to the wider community. The concerns are mainly related to its legality in certain markets and the impact on city life in general.

Consider the example of New York City. For short-term rentals (less than 30 days) in the city, the host must be present on the property, the rooms must be unlocked, and they cannot host more than two guests. While short-term rentals are possible in small buildings (less than three residential units), larger buildings with three or more residential units must be rented at least for 30 days or more. Consequently, many listings on the platform were deemed illegal. To enforce the rules, the city administration enacted a law in 2018, requiring such platforms to provide the hosts' names and addresses to the authorities every month. In August 2018, AirBnB took the city administration to the court arguing that this would breach the privacy of its hosts and endanger their freedom of activity. A federal court blocked the law in Jan 2019, terming it unconstitutional. Similar problems with the legality of AirBnB's listing exist across the globe, in Barcelona, Berlin, Dublin, Paris, Perth, Tokyo, etc. For instance, it was reported[10] in Feb 2020 that only around 250 property owners from Dublin city applied to register their short-term rentals with the council, even though there were more than 7,000 AirBnB properties listed in the area.

France is AirBnB's largest market outside the US, with around 65,000 homes in Paris listed at the time. A French tourism association complained in early 2019 to the European Union, noting that AirBnB was acting as a real estate agent and not complying with EU property rules, thus representing unfair competition to the hotel industry and representing a significant threat to the existing hoteliers in the city. The matter was referred to the European Court of Justice, which issued an opinion in April 2019 stating that AirBnB should be treated as a digital service provider and free to operate across the European Union. The Court noted that AirBnB Ireland (from where AirBnB runs its French website) "may be regarded as an information society service" and should benefit from the EU's free movement of information.[11]

---

10 RTE. (2020). Low compliance rate under laws restricting AirBnB lettings in Dublin city. Available at: https://www.rte.ie/news/dublin/2020/0219/1116267-airbnb-dublin-lettings/.
11 Source: Lexology.com; Available at https://www.lexology.com/library/detail.aspx?g=fe934b09-9da5-41e3-969d-df4f98545f55.

Apart from legality, societal concerns are also coming to the fore.[12] For instance, the boom in AirBnB properties in Dublin and Lisbon is often blamed for the skyrocketing long-term rental market, fuelling the problem of homelessness in the city. In cities like Barcelona or Florence, locals are complaining about the 'touristification' of their city and the loss of cultural capital, for instance, loss of community networks in a locality. In Athens, there have been complaints of too much noise from tourists' late-night parties and their mishandling of the rubbish. Thus, while the guests and hosts might rate each other high on the platform, AirBnB needs to generate trust with the local community.

The appointment of Margaret Richardson as the company's Vice-President of trust in September 2019 was an attempt by the platform to ensure trust and safety among guests, hosts, and the community. The Vice-President of trust is responsible for developing and implementing strategies that would make AirBnB one of the most trusted online communities in the world.

Airbnb in a Covid-19 World

While the company has battled accusations that it drove up rents in many markets and contributed to the nation's housing affordability crisis, the criticism and associated trust issues did not slow the company's explosive growth. It was something else that put a question mark on the future of the company. During the spring of 2020, the Covid-19 pandemic and subsequent travel restrictions caused serious threats to AirBnB.

In the major markets of AirBnB, the effect of the Covid-19 pandemic started manifesting towards the end of February 2020. In the North of Italy, thousands of people were infected. Government agencies like the Centre for Disease Control in the US and European Centre for Disease Prevention and Control recommended avoiding all non-essential international travel. As the pandemic spread to Spain, France, the UK, Ireland, and the US, stricter confinement measures eliminated tourism opportunities. By the end of April 2020, data from the United Nations World Tourism Organisation (UNWTO) showed that 100% of the destinations had restrictions in place.

While AirBnB did not communicate the extent to which it was affected, it is likely that most, if not all the revenues for March, April, and May 2020 dried up. According to AirDNA, an outside tracker of AirBnB listings, hosts saw $1.5 billion in bookings dissipate for March 2020 in the USA alone. By April 2020, AirBnB's valuation plummeted from $31 billion at its 2017 fundraising to $18 billion. The company,

---

12 FT.com. (2019). Are AirBnB investors destroying Europe's cultural capitals? Available at: https://www.ft.com/content/2fe06a7c-cb2a-11e9-af46-b09e8bfe60c0.

which was initially due to go public in 2020, announced on May 5, 2020, that it will slash one-fourth of its workforce – around 1,900 people.

The pandemic represents an immense challenge to the travel industry. It is likely to substantially change our travel habits but perhaps more fundamentally, where we live and how we work. All these changes represent some challenges and some opportunities too for AirBnB.

A report by the Bain Group notes how distance is one of the most fundamental economic factors in today's economy.[13] Traditionally, cities were considered a corner-stone of spatial economics – highly dense urban hubs minimising the cost of moving raw materials, labour, and finished goods. However, thanks to technology, the "cost of distance" is declining in recent times. For instance, big, energy-consuming data centres are usually hosted far from the cities. Such trends are likely to accelerate as a result of the coronavirus crisis. If proximity to one's job location is no longer a signifi-cant factor in deciding where to live, for instance, then the appeal of the suburbs wanes; and remote but digitally connected villages become extremely attractive. AirBnB, which is in the business of leveraging idle capacity, could benefit from this trend. This would however require the company to revise its current approach. The big question is how.

Travel habits are also likely to be affected. Using the hashtag #traveltomorrow, the United Nations specialised agency for tourism (UNWTO) invites people to travel differ-ently in the future. It believes that people may travel to learn from diverse cultures and return home enriched to advance development and promote sustainability. Similarly, it is reported that tourists may not travel as far as they used to and start (re)discovering the world around them instead of far away. Could these concerns and opportunities be integrated by AirBnB in its attempt to build trust with various stakeholders?

Less than 13 years after its inception, AirBnB, which has been a major disruptor in the travel industry, is now being disrupted. The company needs to think of solu-tions to sustain its business model and participate actively in the shaping of a better world, post-Covid-19.

Questions

1. How does AirBnB create value? What is (are) the value proposition(s) of AirBnB? How does it differ from other traditional businesses?
2. Explain the importance of reputational mechanisms in maintaining trust in the context of online C2B2C markets. Explain how AirBnB uses reputational mecha-nisms to ensure and enhance trust between the two sides of the platform.

---

13 Source: https://www.bain.com/insights/spatial-economics-the-declining-cost-of-distance/.

3. How can AirBnB maintain a sustainable tourism platform reputation and address the concerns over its alleged negative impact discussed in the case?

4. What are the possible behavioural changes of business and personal travellers resulting from the covid-19 pandemic? How can Airbnb address these long-term changes? Should it be reconsidering its target audience, its value proposition, or its business model? How?

Appendix 1 – Founders' Profiles

Source: AirBnB.com; Available at https://news.airbnb.com/about-us/.

Brian Chesky is the co-founder, head of community, and CEO of AirBnB, which he started with Joe Gebbia and Nathan Blecharczyk in 2008. Originally from New York, Brian graduated from the Rhode Island School of Design, where he received a Bachelor of Fine Arts degree in industrial design. Brian sets the company's strategy to connect people to unique travel experiences and drives AirBnB's mission to create a world where anyone can belong anywhere.

Joe Gebbia is the co-founder and CPO of AirBnB, serving on the board of directors and executive staff while leading Samara, AirBnB's in-house design and innovation studio. Like Brian, he is also an alumnus of the Rhode Island School of Design, where he earned dual degrees in graphic design and industrial design. An entrepreneur from an early age, AirBnB's ground breaking service began in his San Francisco apartment. He is involved in crafting the company culture, shaping the design aesthetic, and innovating future growth opportunities. Joe has spoken globally about both entrepreneurship and design and received numerous distinctions such as the Inc. 30 under 30 and Fortune 40 under 40. Gebbia now serves on the institution's board of trustees.

Nathan Blecharczyk is the co-founder, chief strategy officer, and chairman of AirBnB China. Nathan became an entrepreneur in his youth, running a business while he was in high school that sold to clients in more than 20 countries. He earned a degree in computer science from Harvard University and held several engineering positions before co-founding AirBnB. Nathan plays a leading role in driving key strategic initiatives across the global business. Previously, he oversaw the creation of AirBnB's engineering, data science, and performance marketing teams.

Appendix 2: AirBnB's Development Story

Based on data available at https://news.airbnb.com/fast-facts/.

2007 Brian Chesky and Joe Gebbia use air-beds to make rent money when hotels are sold out

2008 Officail launch; Formal website; Founders raise $30,000 by selling election-themed cereals

2009 Name changed to Airbnb; Expands beyond rooms to include apartments and houses

2010 Launch iPhone app and Instant Book feature

2011 International expansion begins with German office

2012 Introduces $1m Host Guarantee to protect against property damage

2013 Moves headquarters to 888 Brannan Street in San Francisco

2014 100,000 guests during Rio World Cup; 1,500 hosts attend Airbnb Open in San Francisco

2015 Offivial alternative accommodation supplier for Rio Olympics; 6,000 hosts attend Paris Arirbanb Open

2016 Launches Trips; 7,000 people attend Airbnb Open in Loss Angeles

2017 Expands Trips to 20 more cities; Launches Chinese brand

2018 Launches Airbnb Plus; Celebrates 10 years

2019 Acquires Hotel Tonight to provide options when Hosts unavailable

Appendix 3: AirBnB Funding Rounds

Funding type	Date	Amount raised	Post-money valuation
Seed	Jan 2009	$20 k	$2.5 m
Seed	Apr 2009	$615 k	
Series A	Nov 2010	$7.2 m	$70 m
Series B-1	Jul 2011	$114.9 m	$1.3 b
Series B-2	Jul 2011	$2.1 m	
Series C	Oct 2013	$200 m	$2.9 b
Series D	Apr 2014	$519.7 m	$10.5 b
Series E-1	Jun 2015	$1.6 b	$25.5 b
Series E-2	Nov 2015	$100 m	
Debt	Jul 2016	$1 b	

(continued)

Funding type	Date	Amount raised	Post-money valuation
Series F	Sept 2016	$1 b	$31 b
Unattributed	Apr 2019	$201.6 m	
Unattributed	Aug 2019	$25.9 m	

Source: https://craft.co/airbnb/funding-rounds.

Appendix 4: AirBnB Revenue over the Years

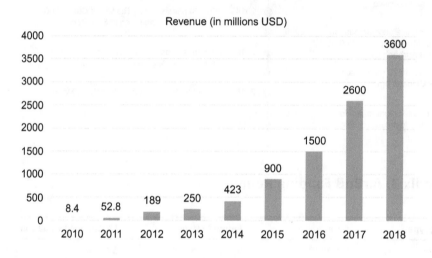

Revenue (in millions USD)

List of Figures

Index

Printed in the USA
CPSIA information can be obtained
at www.ICGtesting.com
LVHW080012161123
763915LV00008B/70

9 783110 762419